WHAT'S COOKING
chocolate

Jacqueline Bellefontaine

p

This is a Parragon Book
This edition published in 2000

Parragon
Queen Street House
4 Queen Street
Bath BA1 1HE, UK

ISBN: 0-75253-847-0 (Paperback)
ISBN: 0-75253-853-5 (Hardback)

Printed in Indonesia

Produced by Haldane Mason, London

Acknowledgements
Art Director: Ron Samuels
Editorial Director: Sydney Francis
Editorial Consultant: Christopher Fagg
Managing Editor: Jo-Anne Cox
Editor: Felicity Jackson
Design: Digital Artworks Partnership Ltd
Photography: St John Asprey
Home Economist: Jacqueline Bellefontaine

Note
Cup measurements in this book are for American cups.
Tablespoons are assumed to be 15 ml. Unless otherwise stated,
milk is assumed to be full fat, eggs are medium
and pepper is freshly ground black pepper.

The equipment on pages 20-21, 30-31, 40-41, 68-69, 90-91, 156-157 and 212-213
was kindley supplied by Divertimenti, 139 Fulham Rd, London SW3

Contents

Introduction

Chocolate is one of life's luxuries and one of the few that we can all afford. This book contains all of the recipes you need to enjoy this luxury at any time of the day. For example, you could wake up to Pain au Chocolat, or have a tasty chocolate biscuit with morning coffee. You could indulge in a hot chocolate pudding at lunch time, have a sumptuous slice of chocolate cake with afternoon tea, luxuriate with a rich chocolate dessert as part of the evening meal and round off the end of the day with a hot chocolate toddy. Whilst this might seem to be taking things too far, even for the most hardened chocoholic, why not tempt yourself with a perfect chocolate treat now and then. Go on spoil yourself!

Chocolate is produced from the beans of the cacao tree, which originated in South America, but now grows in Africa, the West Indies, the tropical parts of America and the Far East. Cacao beans are large pods – once harvested, both the pulp from the pods and the bean are allowed to ferment in the sun. The pulp evaporates and the bean develops it's chocolatey flavour. The outer skin is then removed and the beans are left in the sun for a little longer or roasted. Finally, they are shelled and the kernels are used for making cocoa and chocolate.

The kernels have to be ground and processed to produce a thick mixture or paste called "cocoa solids" and it is this that we refer to when gauging the quality of chocolate. The cocoa solids are then pressed to remove some of the fat – 'cocoa butter'. They are then further processed to produce the product that we know and love as chocolate.

STORING CHOCOLATE

Store chocolate in a cool, dry place away from direct heat or sunlight. Most chocolate can be stored for about 1 year. It can be stored in the refrigerator, but make sure it is well wrapped as it will pick up flavours from other foods. Chocolate decorations can be stored in airtight containers and interleaved with non-stick baking parchment. Dark chocolate will keep for 4 weeks and milk and white chocolate for 2 weeks.

MELTING CHOCOLATE

Chocolate should not be melted over direct heat, except when melted with other ingredients and even then the heat should be very low.

Break the chocolate into small, equal-sized pieces and place them in a heatproof bowl. Place over a pan of hot water, making sure the base is not in contact with the water. Once the chocolate starts to melt, stir gently and if necessary leave over the water a little longer. No drops of water or steam should come into contact with the melted chocolate as it will solidify.

To melt chocolate in the microwave, break the chocolate into small pieces and place in microwave-proof bowl. Timing will vary according to the type and quantity of chocolate. As a guide, melt 125 g/4½ oz dark chocolate on High for 2 minutes and white or milk chocolate for 2-3 minutes on Medium. Stir the chocolate and leave to stand for a few minutes, then stir again. Return to the microwave for a further 30 seconds if necessary.

SETTING CHOCOLATE

Chocolate sets best at 65°F/18°C although it will set (more slowly) in a slightly hotter room. If possible set chocolate for decorations in a cool room. If set in the refrigerator it may develop a white bloom.

TYPES OF CHOCOLATE

Dark Chocolate *can contain anything from 30% to 75% cocoa solids. It has a slightly sweet flavour and a dark colour. It is the chocolate most used in cooking. For everyday cooking and the majority of these recipes calling for dark chocolate, choose one with around 50% cocoa solids. However, dark chocolate with a higher cocoa solid content will give a richer more intense flavour. This chocolate is often called luxury or continental chocolate and has a cocoa solid content of between 70-75%. Occasionally it is essential to use a better chocolate and I have indicated in the individual recipes where this is the case.*

Milk Chocolate, *as it's name suggests, contains milk and has a lovely creamy, mild and sweet flavour. It is mostly used as an eating chocolate, rather than in cooking. However it does have it's place in chocolate cookery, especially for decorations and when a milder, creamy flavour is required. It is more sensitive to heat than dark chocolate so care must be taken when melting it.*

White Chocolate *contains a lower cocoa butter content and cocoa solids. It can be quite temperamental when used in cooking. Always choose a luxury cooking white chocolate to avoid problems and take great care not to overheat when melting. White chocolate is useful for colour contrast especially when decorating cakes.*

Couverture, *although this is the preferred chocolate for professionals (it retains a high gloss after melting and cooling) it requires tempering and is only available from specialist suppliers and has therefore not been used in this book.*

Chocolate-flavoured Cake Covering *is an inferior product not generally used by true chocolate lovers. However it has a higher fat content making it easier to handle when making some decorations, such as curls or caraque. If you do not want to compromise the flavour too much, but have difficulty making the decorations with pure chocolate, try adding a few squares of chocolate-flavoured cake covering to a good quality chocolate.*

Chocolate Chips *are available in dark, milk and white chocolate varieties and are used for baking and decoration.*

Cocoa Powder *is the powder left after the cocoa butter has been pressed from the roasted and ground beans. It is unsweetened and bitter in flavour. It gives a good, strong chocolate flavour when used in cooking.*

Dark Chocolate

Milk Chocolate

White Chocolate

Chocolate Chips

Cakes & Gateaux

It is hard to resist the pleasure of a sumptuous piece of chocolate cake and no chocolate book would be complete without a selection of family cakes and gateaux – there are plenty to choose from in this chapter. You can spend several indulgent hours in the kitchen making that perfect extravagant gateau or pop into the kitchen to knock up a quick cake for afternoon tea, the choice is yours. The more experimental amongst you can vary the fillings or decorations used according to what takes your fancy.

Alternatively, follow our easy step-by-step instructions and look at our glossy pictures to guide you to perfect results. The gateaux in this book will be just at home on the dessert table – they are a feast for the eyes and will keep all hardened chocoholics in ecstasy. The family cakes are ideal for those who find a slice of chocolate cake comforting at any time, as many of them are made with surprising ease. So next time you feel like an indulgent slice of melt-in-the-mouth chocolate cake look no further.'

Chocolate Almond Cake

Chocolate and almonds complement each other perfectly in this delicious cake.
Be warned, one slice will never be enough!

Serves 8-10

INGREDIENTS

175 g/6 oz dark chocolate
175 g/6 oz/^{3}/4 cup butter
125 g/4^1/2 oz caster (superfine) sugar
4 eggs, separated
^{1}/4 tsp cream of tartar
50 g/1^3/4 oz/^{1}/3 cup self-raising flour

125 g/4^1/2 oz/1^1/4 cups ground
almonds
1 tsp almond flavouring (extract)

TOPPING:
125 g/4^1/2 oz milk chocolate
25 g/1 oz/2 tbsp butter

4 tbsp double (heavy) cream

TO DECORATE:
25 g/1 oz/2 tbsp toasted flaked
almonds
25 g/1 oz dark chocolate, melted

1 Lightly grease and line the base of a 23 cm/9 inch round springform tin (pan). Break the chocolate into small pieces and place in a small pan with the butter. Heat gently, stirring until melted and well combined.

2 Place 100 g/3^1/2 oz/7 tbsp of the caster (superfine) sugar in a bowl with the egg yolks and whisk until pale and creamy. Add the melted chocolate mixture, beating until well combined.

3 Sieve (strain) the cream of tartar and flour together and fold into the chocolate mixture with the ground almonds and almond flavouring (extract).

4 Whisk the egg whites in a bowl until standing in soft peaks. Add the remaining caster (superfine) sugar and whisk for about 2 minutes by hand, or 45-60 seconds, if using an electric whisk, until thick and glossy. Fold the egg whites into the chocolate mixture

and spoon into the tin (pan). Bake in a preheated oven, 190°C/375°F/ Gas Mark 5, for 40 minutes until just springy to the touch. Let cool.

5 Heat the topping ingredients in a bowl over a pan of hot water. Remove from the heat and beat for 2 minutes. Let chill for 30 minutes. Transfer the cake to a plate and spread with the topping. Scatter with the almonds and drizzle with melted chocolate. Leave to set for 2 hours before serving.

Chocolate Tray Bake

This is a good family cake that keeps well. Baked in a shallow rectangular cake tin (pan), it is ideal for selling at a cake stall or charity coffee mornings.

Serves 15

INGREDIENTS

350 g/12 oz/3 cups self-raising flour, sieved (strained)

3 tbsp cocoa powder, sieved (strained)

225 g/8 oz/1 cup caster (superfine) sugar

225 g/8 oz/1 cup soft margarine

4 eggs, beaten

4 tbsp milk

50 g/1³/₄ oz/¹/₃ cup milk chocolate chips

50 g/1³/₄ oz/¹/₃ cup dark chocolate chips

50 g/1³/₄ oz/¹/₃ cup white chocolate chips

icing (confectioners') sugar, to dust

1 Grease a 33 × 24 × 5 cm/ 13 × 9 × 2 inch cake tin (pan) with a little butter or margarine.

2 Place all of the ingredients except for the chocolate chips and icing (confectioners') sugar in a large mixing bowl and beat together until smooth.

3 Beat in the milk, dark and white chocolate chips.

4 Spoon the mixture into the prepared cake tin (pan) and level the top. Bake in a preheated oven, 180°C/350°F/Gas Mark 4, for 30–40 minutes until risen and springy to the touch. Leave to cool in the tin (pan).

5 Once cool, dust with icing (confectioners') sugar. Cut into squares to serve.

COOK'S TIP

If liked, serve warm with whipped cream for a delicious dessert.

COOK'S TIP

The cake can be frozen, wrapped well in the tin (pan), for 2 months. Defrost at room temperature.

VARIATION

For an attractive finish, cut thin strips of paper and lay in a criss-cross pattern on top of the cake. Dust with icing (confectioners') sugar, then remove the paper strips.

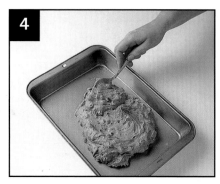

Low-fat Chocolate & Pineapple Cake

Decorated with thick yogurt and canned pineapple, this is a low-fat cake, but it is by no means lacking in flavour.

Serves 9

INGREDIENTS

150 g/5$^{1}/_{2}$ oz/$^{2}/_{3}$ cup low-fat spread
125 g/4$^{1}/_{2}$ oz caster (superfine) sugar
100 g/3$^{1}/_{2}$ oz/$^{3}/_{4}$ cup self-raising flour, sieved (strained)
3 tbsp cocoa powder, sieved (strained)

1$^{1}/_{2}$ tsp baking powder
2 eggs
225g/8 oz can pineapple pieces in natural juice
125 ml/4 fl oz/$^{1}/_{2}$ cup low-fat thick natural yogurt

about 1 tbsp icing (confectioners') sugar
grated chocolate, to decorate

1 Lightly grease a 20 cm/8 inch square cake tin (pan).

2 Place the low-fat spread, caster (superfine) sugar, flour, cocoa powder, baking powder and eggs in a large mixing bowl. Beat with a wooden spoon or electric hand whisk until smooth.

3 Pour the cake mixture into the prepared tin (pan) and level the surface. Bake in a preheated oven, 190°C/325°F/Gas Mark 5, for 20-25 minutes or until springy to the touch. Leave to cool slightly in the tin (pan) before transferring to a wire rack to cool completely.

4 Drain the pineapple, chop the pineapple pieces and drain again. Reserve a little pineapple for decoration, then stir the rest into the yogurt and sweeten to taste with icing (confectioners') sugar.

5 Spread the pineapple and yogurt mixture over the cake and decorate with the reserved pineapple pieces. Sprinkle with the grated chocolate.

COOK'S TIP

Store the cake, undecorated, in an airtight container for up to 3 days. Once decorated, refrigerate and use within 2 days.

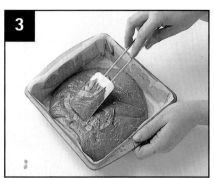

Chocolate & Orange Cake

An all-time favourite combination of flavours means this cake is ideal for a tea-time treat.
Omit the icing, if preferred, and sprinkle with icing (confectioners') sugar.

Serves 8–10

INGREDIENTS

175 g/6 oz/$^3/_4$ cup caster (superfine) sugar
175 g/6 oz/$^3/_4$ cup butter or block margarine
3 eggs, beaten

175 g/6 oz/1$^1/_2$ cups self-raising flour, sieved (strained)
2 tbsp cocoa powder, sieved (strained)
2 tbsp milk
3 tbsp orange juice

grated rind of $^1/_2$ orange

ICING:
175 g/6 oz/1 cup icing (confectioners') sugar
2 tbsp orange juice

1 Lightly grease a 20 cm/8 inch deep round cake tin (pan).

2 Beat together the sugar and butter or margarine in a bowl until light and fluffy. Gradually add the eggs, beating well after each addition. Carefully fold in the flour.

3 Divide the mixture in half. Add the cocoa powder and milk to one half, stirring until well combined. Flavour the other half with the orange juice and rind.

4 Place spoonfuls of each mixture into the prepared tin (pan) and swirl together with a skewer, to create a marbled effect. Bake in a preheated oven, 190°C/375°F/Gas Mark 5, for 25 minutes or until springy to the touch.

5 Leave the cake to cool in the tin (pan) for a few minutes before transferring to a wire rack to cool completely.

6 To make the icing, sift the icing (confectioners') sugar into a mixing bowl and mix in enough of the orange juice to form a smooth icing. Spread the icing over the top of the cake and leave to set before serving.

VARIATION

Add 2 tablespoons of rum or brandy to the chocolate mixture instead of the milk. The cake also works well when flavoured with grated lemon rind and juice instead of the orange.

Family Chocolate Cake

A simple to make family cake ideal for an everyday treat. Keep the decoration as simple as you like – you could use a bought icing or filling, if liked.

Serves 8-10

INGREDIENTS

125 g/4^1/$_2$ oz/^{1}/$_2$ cup soft margarine
125 g/4^1/$_2$ oz/^{1}/$_2$ cup caster
   (superfine) sugar
2 eggs
1 tbsp golden (light corn) syrup
125 g/4^1/$_2$ oz/1 cup self-raising flour,
   sieved (strained)

2 tbsp cocoa powder, sieved
(strained)

FILLING AND TOPPING:
50 g/1^3/$_4$ oz/^{1}/$_4$ cup icing
(confectioners') sugar, sieved
(strained)

25 g/1 oz/2 tbsp butter
100 g/3^1/$_2$ oz white or milk cooking
   chocolate
a little milk or white chocolate,
   melted (optional)

1 Lightly grease two 18 cm/7 inch shallow cake tins (pans).

2 Place all of the ingredients for the cake in a large mixing bowl and beat with a wooden spoon or electric hand whisk to form a smooth mixture.

3 Divide the mixture between the prepared tins (pans) and level the tops. Bake in a preheated oven, 190°C/325F/Gas Mark 5, for 20 minutes or until springy to the touch. Cool for a few minutes in the tins (pans) before transferring to a wire rack to cool completely.

4 To make the filling, beat the icing (confectioners') sugar and butter together in a bowl until light and fluffy. Melt the cooking chocolate and beat half into the icing mixture. Use the filling to sandwich the 2 cakes together.

5 Spread the remaining melted cooking chocolate over the top of the cake. Pipe circles of contrasting melted milk or white chocolate and feather into the cooking chocolate with a cocktail stick (toothpick), if liked. Leave to set before serving.

COOK'S TIP

Ensure that you eat this cake on the day of baking, as it does not keep well.

Chocolate & Vanilla Loaf Cake

An old-fashioned favourite, this cake will keep well if stored in an airtight container or wrapped in foil in a cool place.

Serves 10

INGREDIENTS

175 g/6 oz/³/₄ cup caster (superfine) sugar
175 g/6 oz/³/₄ cup soft margarine
¹/₂ tsp vanilla flavouring (extract)

3 eggs
225 g/8 oz/2 cups self-raising flour, sieved (strained)
50 g/1³/₄ oz dark chocolate

icing (confectioners') sugar, to dust

1 Lightly grease a 450 g/1 lb loaf tin (pan).

2 Beat together the sugar and soft margarine in a bowl until light and fluffy.

3 Beat in the vanilla flavouring (extract). Gradually add the eggs, beating well after each addition. Carefully fold in the self-raising flour.

4 Divide the mixture in half. Melt the dark chocolate and stir into one half of the mixture until well combined.

5 Place the vanilla mixture in the tin (pan) and level the top. Spread the chocolate layer over the vanilla layer.

6 Bake in a preheated oven, 190°C/375°F/Gas Mark 5, for 30 minutes or until springy to the touch.

7 Leave to cool in the tin (pan) for a few minutes before transferring to a wire rack to cool completely.

8 Serve the cake dusted with icing (confectioners') sugar.

VARIATION

If liked, the mixtures can be marbled together with a cocktail stick (toothpick).

COOK'S TIP

Freeze the cake undecorated for up to 2 months. Defrost at room temperature.

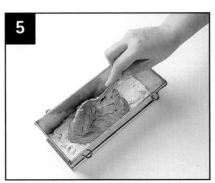

Chocolate Tea Bread

*What better in the afternoon than to sit down with a cup of tea
and a slice of tea bread, and when it's made of chocolate it's even better.*

Serves 10

INGREDIENTS

175 g/6 oz/³/₄ cup butter, softened
100 g/3¹/₂ oz light muscovado sugar
4 eggs, lightly beaten

225 g/8 oz dark chocolate chips
100 g/3¹/₂ oz/¹/₂ cup raisins
50 g/1³/₄ oz/¹/₂ cup chopped walnuts

finely grated rind of 1 orange
225 g/8 oz/2 cups self-raising flour

1 Lightly grease a 900 g/2 lb loaf tin (pan) and line the base with baking parchment.

2 Cream together the butter and sugar in a bowl until light and fluffy.

3 Gradually add the eggs, beating well after each addition. If the mixture begins to curdle, beat in 1–2 tablespoons of the flour.

4 Stir in the chocolate chips, raisins, walnuts and orange rind. Sieve (strain) the flour and carefully fold it into the mixture.

5 Spoon the mixture into the prepared loaf tin (pan) and make a slight dip in the centre of the top with the back of a spoon.

6 Bake in a preheated oven, 170°C/325°F/Gas Mark 3, for 1 hour or until a fine skewer inserted into the centre of the loaf comes out clean.

7 Leave to cool in the tin (pan) for 5 minutes, before carefully turning out and leaving on a wire rack to cool completely.

8 Serve the tea bread cut into thin slices.

VARIATION

Use white or milk chocolate chips instead of dark chocolate chips, or a mixture of all three, if desired. Dried cranberries instead of the raisins also work well in this recipe.

COOK'S TIP

This tea bread can be frozen, well wrapped, for up to 3 months. Defrost at room temperature.

Apricot & Chocolate Ring

*A tasty tea bread in the shape of a ring. You could use sultanas
instead of the apricots, if preferred.*

Serves 12

INGREDIENTS

75 g/2³/₄ oz/¹/₃ cup butter, diced
450 g/1 lb/4 cups self-raising flour,
　sieved (strained)
50 g/1³/₄ oz/4 tbsp caster (superfine)
　sugar

2 eggs, beaten
150 ml/¹/₄ pint/²/₃ cup milk

FILLING AND DECORATION:
25 g/1 oz/2 tbsp butter, melted

150 g/5¹/₂ oz ready-to-eat dried
　apricots, chopped
100 g/3¹/₂ oz dark chocolate chips
1-2 tbsp milk, to glaze
25 g/1 oz dark chocolate, melted

1 Grease a 25 cm/10 inch round cake tin (pan) and line the base with baking parchment.

2 Rub the butter into the flour until the mixture resembles fine breadcrumbs. Stir in the caster (superfine) sugar, eggs and milk to form a soft dough.

3 Roll out the dough on a lightly floured surface to form a 35 cm/14 inch square.

4 Brush the melted butter over the surface of the dough. Mix together the apricots and chocolate chips and spread them over the dough to within 2.5 cm/1 inch of the top and bottom.

5 Roll up the dough tightly, like a Swiss roll, and cut it into 2.5 cm/1 inch slices. Stand the slices in a ring around the edge of the prepared tin (pan) at a slight tilt. Brush with a little milk.

6 Bake in a preheated oven, 180°C/350°F/Gas Mark 4, for 30 minutes or until cooked and golden. Leave to cool in the tin (pan) for about 15 minutes, then transfer to a wire rack to cool.

7 Drizzle the melted chocolate over the ring, to decorate.

COOK'S TIP

This cake is best served very fresh, ideally on the day it is made. It is fabulous served slightly warm.

Chocolate Fruit Loaf

A very moreish loaf that smells divine whilst cooking. It is best eaten warm.

Serves 10

INGREDIENTS

350 g/12 oz/3 cups strong white
    flour
25 g/1 oz/$^1/_4$ cup cocoa powder
25 g/1 oz/5 tsp caster (superfine)
    sugar
6 g sachet easy blend yeast
$^1/_4$ tsp salt
225 ml/8 fl oz/1 cup tepid water

25 g/1 oz/2 tbsp butter, melted
75 g/2$^3/_4$ oz/5 tbsp glacé (candied)
    cherries, chopped roughly
75 g/2$^3/_4$ oz/$^1/_2$ cup dark chocolate
    chips
50 g/1$^3/_4$ oz/$^1/_3$ cup sultanas (golden
    raisins)

75 g/2$^3/_4$ oz no-soak dried apricots,
    roughly chopped

GLAZE:
1 tbsp caster (superfine) sugar
1 tbsp water

1 Lightly grease a 900 g/2 lb loaf tin (pan). Sieve (strain) the flour and cocoa into a large mixing bowl. Stir in the sugar, yeast and salt.

2 Mix together the tepid water and butter. Make a well in the centre of the dry ingredients and add the liquid. Mix well with a wooden spoon, then use your hands to bring the dough together. Turn out on to a lightly floured surface and knead for 5 minutes, until a smooth elastic dough forms. Return to a clean bowl, cover with a damp tea towel and leave to rise in a warm place for about 1 hour or until doubled in size.

3 Turn the dough out on to a floured surface and knead for 5 minutes. Roll out to a rectangle about 1 cm/$^1/_2$ inch thick and the same width as the length of the tin (pan). Scatter the cherries, chocolate chips, sultanas (golden raisins) and chopped apricots over the dough. Carefully roll up the dough, like a Swiss roll, enclosing the filling. Transfer to the loaf tin (pan), cover with a damp tea towel and leave to rise for 20 minutes or until the top of the dough is level with the top of the tin (pan).

4 To make the glaze, mix together the sugar and water, then brush it over the top of the loaf. Bake in a preheated oven, 200°C/400°F/Gas Mark 6, for 30 minutes or until well risen. Serve.

Mocha Layer Cake

*Chocolate cake and a creamy coffee-flavoured filling
are combined in this delicious mocha cake.*

Serves 8–10

INGREDIENTS

200 g/7^3/4 oz/1 cup self-raising flour
^{1}/4 tsp baking powder
4 tbsp cocoa powder
100 g/3^1/2 oz/7 tbsp caster
   (superfine) sugar
2 eggs
2 tbsp golden (light corn) syrup

150 ml/^{1}/4 pint/^{2}/3 cup sunflower oil
150 ml/^{1}/4 pint/^{2}/3 cup milk

FILLING:
1 tsp instant coffee
1 tbsp boiling water
300 ml/^{1}/2 pint/1^1/4 cups double
   (heavy) cream

25 g/1 oz/2 tbsp icing
(confectioners') sugar

TO DECORATE:
50 g/1^3/4 oz flock chocolate
chocolate caraque (see page 208)
icing (confectioners') sugar, to dust

1 Lightly grease three 18 cm/ 7 inch cake tins (pans).

2 Sieve (strain) the flour, baking powder and cocoa powder into a large mixing bowl. Stir in the sugar. Make a well in the centre and stir in the eggs, syrup, oil and milk. Beat with a wooden spoon, gradually mixing in the dry ingredients to make a smooth batter. Divide the mixture between the prepared tins (pans).

3 Bake in a preheated oven, 180°C/350°F/Gas Mark 4, for 35-45 minutes or until springy to the touch. Leave in the tins (pans) for 5 minutes, then turn out on to a wire rack to cool completely.

4 Dissolve the instant coffee in the boiling water and place in a bowl with the cream and icing (confectioners') sugar. Whip until the cream is just holding it's shape. Use half of the cream to sandwich

the 3 cakes together. Spread the remaining cream over the top and sides of the cake. Lightly press the flock chocolate into the cream around the edge of the cake.

5 Transfer to a serving plate. Lay the caraque over the top of the cake. Cut a few thin strips of baking parchment and place on top of the caraque. Dust lightly with icing (confectioners') sugar, then carefully remove the paper. Serve.

Chocolate Lamington Bar Cake

This cake is based on the famous Australian Lamington cake, named after Lord Lamington,
a former Governor of Queensland, which has chocolate icing covered with coconut.

Serves 8-10

INGREDIENTS

175 g/6 oz/^{3}/$_4$ cup butter or block
 margarine
175 g/6 oz/^{3}/$_4$ cup caster (superfine)
 sugar
3 eggs, lightly beaten
150 g/5^1/$_2$ oz/1^1/$_4$ cups self-raising
 flour

2 tbsp cocoa powder
125 g/4^1/$_2$ oz/^{3}/$_4$ cup icing
 (confectioners') sugar
50 g/1^3/$_4$ oz dark chocolate, broken
 into pieces
5 tbsp milk
1 tsp butter

about 8 tbsp desiccated (shredded)
 coconut
150 ml/^{1}/$_4$ pint double (heavy)
 cream), whipped

1 Lightly grease a 450 g/1 lb loaf tin (pan) – preferably a long, thin tin (pan) about 7.5 × 25 cm/3 × 10 inches.

2 Cream together the butter and sugar in a bowl until light and fluffy. Gradually add the eggs, beating well after each addition. Sieve (strain) together the flour and cocoa. Fold into the mixture.

3 Pour the mixture into the prepared tin (pan) and level the top. Bake in a preheated oven, 180°C/350°F/Gas Mark 4, for 40 minutes or until springy to the touch. Leave to cool for 5 minutes in the tin (pan), then turn out on to a wire rack to cool completely.

4 Place the chocolate, milk and butter in a heatproof bowl set over a pan of hot water. Stir until the chocolate has melted. Add the icing (confectioners') sugar and beat until smooth. Leave to cool until the icing is thick enough to spread, then spread it all over the cake. Sprinkle with the desiccated (shredded) coconut and allow the icing to set.

5 Cut a V-shape wedge from the top of the cake. Put the cream in a piping bag fitted with a plain or star nozzle (tip). Pipe the cream down the centre of the wedge and replace the wedge of cake on top of the cream. Pipe another line of cream down either side of the wedge of cake. Serve.

Rich Chocolate Layer Cake

Thin layers of delicious light chocolate cake sandwiched together with a rich chocolate icing.

Serves 10–12

INGREDIENTS

7 eggs
200 g/7 oz/1³/4 cups caster
   (superfine) sugar
150 g/5¹/2 oz/1¹/4 cups plain (all-
   purpose) flour
50 g/1³/4 oz/¹/2 cup cocoa powder
50 g/1³/4 oz/4 tbsp butter, melted

FILLING:
200 g/7 oz dark chocolate
125 g/4¹/2 oz/¹/2 cup butter
50 g/1³/4 oz/4 tbsp icing
   (confectioners') sugar

TO DECORATE:
75 g/2³/4 oz/10 tbsp toasted flaked
   almonds, crushed lightly
small chocolate curls (see page 214)
   or grated chocolate

1 Grease a deep 23 cm/9 inch square cake tin (pan) and line the base with baking parchment.

2 Whisk the eggs and caster (superfine) sugar in a mixing bowl with an electric whisk for about 10 minutes, or until the mixture is very light and foamy and the whisk leaves a trail that lasts a few seconds when lifted.

3 Sieve (strain) the flour and cocoa together and fold half into the mixture. Drizzle over the melted butter and fold in the rest of the flour and cocoa. Pour into the prepared tin (pan) and bake in a preheated oven, 180°C/350°F/ Gas Mark 4, for 30-35 minutes or until springy to the touch. Leave to cool slightly, then remove from the tin (pan) and cool completely on a wire rack. Wash and dry the tin (pan) and return the cake to it.

4 To make the filling, melt the chocolate and butter together, then remove from the heat. Stir in the icing (confectioners') sugar, leave to cool, then beat until thick enough to spread.

5 Halve the cake lengthways and cut each half into 3 layers. Sandwich the layers together with three-quarters of the chocolate filling. Spread the remainder over the cake and mark a wavy pattern on the top. Press the almonds on to the sides. Decorate with chocolate curls or grated chocolate.

Chocolate & Mango Layer

Peaches can be used instead of mangoes for this deliciously moist cake, if you prefer. If the top of the cake is very domed, cut a piece off, then turn the cake upside down so that you have a flat surface to decorate.

Serves 12

INGREDIENTS

50 g/1³/₄ oz/¹/₂ cup cocoa powder
150 ml/¹/₄ pint/²/₃ cup boiling water
6 large eggs
350 g/12 oz/1¹/₂ cups caster
   (superfine) sugar

300 g/10¹/₂ oz/2¹/₂ cups self-raising
   flour
2 x 400 g/14 oz cans mango
1 tsp cornflour (cornstarch)

425 ml/³/₄ pint/generous 1³/₄ cups
   double (heavy) cream
75 g/2³/₄ oz dark flock chocolate or
   grated chocolate

1 Grease a deep 23 cm/9 inch round cake tin (pan) and line the base with baking parchment.

2 Place the cocoa powder in a small bowl and gradually add the boiling water; blend to form a smooth paste.

3 Place the eggs and caster (superfine) sugar in a mixing bowl and whisk until the mixture is very light and foamy and the whisk leaves a trail that lasts a few seconds when lifted. Fold in the cocoa mixture. Sieve (strain) the flour and fold into the mixture.

4 Pour the mixture into the tin (pan) and level the top. Bake in a preheated oven, 170°C/325°F/ Gas Mark 3, for about 1 hour or until springy to the touch.

5 Leave to cool in the tin (pan) for a few minutes then turn out and cool completely on a wire rack. Peel off the lining paper and cut the cake into 3 layers.

6 Drain the mangoes and place a quarter of them in a food processor and purée until smooth. Mix the cornflour (cornstarch) with about 3 tbsp of the mango juice to

form a smooth paste. Add to the mango purée. Transfer to a small pan and heat gently, stirring until the purée thickens. Leave to cool.

7 Chop the remaining mango. Whip the cream and reserve about one quarter. Fold the mango into the remaining cream and use to sandwich the layers of cake together. Place on a serving plate. Spread some of the remaining cream around the side of the cake. Press the flock or grated chocolate lightly into the cream. Pipe cream rosettes around the top. Spread the mango purée over the centre.

Devil's Food Cake

This is an American classic, consisting of a rich melt-in-the-mouth chocolate cake that has a citrus-flavoured frosting.

Serves 8

INGREDIENTS

100 g/3^1/$_2$ oz dark chocolate
250 g/9 oz/2^1/$_4$ cups self-raising flour
1 tsp bicarbonate of soda (baking soda)
225 g/8 oz/1 cup butter

400 g/14 oz/2^2/$_3$ cups dark muscovado sugar
1 tsp vanilla flavouring (extract)
3 eggs
125 ml/4 fl oz/^{1}/$_2$ cup buttermilk
225 ml/8 fl oz/2 cups boiling water

FROSTING:
300 g/10^1/$_2$ oz/1^1/$_3$ cups caster (superfine) sugar
2 egg whites
1 tbsp lemon juice
3 tbsp orange juice
candied orange peel, to decorate

1 Lightly grease two 20 cm/ 8 inch shallow round cake tins (pans) and line the bases. Melt the chocolate in a pan. Sieve (strain) the flour and bicarbonate of soda (baking soda) together.

2 Beat the butter and sugar in a bowl until pale and fluffy. Beat in the vanilla flavouring (extract) and the eggs, one at a time and beating well after each addition. Add a little flour if the mixture begins to curdle.

3 Fold the melted chocolate into the mixture until well blended. Gradually fold in the remaining flour, then stir in the buttermilk and boiling water.

4 Divide the mixture between the tins (pans) and level the tops. Bake in a preheated oven, 190°C/375°F/Gas Mark 5, for 30 minutes until springy to the touch. Leave to cool in the tin (pan) for 5 minutes, then transfer to a wire rack to cool completely.

5 Place the frosting ingredients in a large bowl set over a pan of gently simmering water. Whisk, preferably with an electric beater, until thickened and forming soft peaks. Remove from the heat and whisk until the mixture is cool.

6 Sandwich the 2 cakes together with a little of the frosting, then spread the remainder over the sides and top of the cake, swirling it as you do so. Decorate with the candied orange peel.

Chocolate Passion Cake

What could be nicer than passion cake with added chocolate?
Rich and moist, this cake is fabulous with afternoon tea.

Serves 10–12

INGREDIENTS

5 eggs
150 g/5^1/2 oz/^{2}/3 cup caster (superfine) sugar
150 g/5^1/2 oz/1^1/4 cups plain (all-purpose) flour

40 g/1^1/2 oz/^{1}/3 cup cocoa powder
175 g/6 oz carrots, peeled and finely grated
50 g/1^3/4 oz/^{1}/2 cup chopped walnuts
2 tbsp sunflower oil

350 g/12 oz medium fat soft cheese
175 g/6 oz/1 cup icing (confectioners') sugar
175 g/6 oz milk or dark chocolate, melted

1 Lightly grease and line the base of a 20 cm/8 inch deep round cake tin (pan).

2 Place the eggs and sugar in a large mixing bowl set over a pan of gently simmering water and whisk until very thick. Lift the whisk up and let the mixture drizzle back – it will leave a trail for a few seconds when thick enough.

3 Remove the bowl from the heat. Sieve (strain) the flour and cocoa powder into the bowl and carefully fold in. Fold in the carrots, walnuts and oil until just combined.

4 Pour into the prepared tin (pan) and bake in a preheated oven, 190°C/375°F/Gas Mark 5, for 45 minutes or until well risen and springy to the touch. Leave to cool slightly then turn out on to a wire rack to cool completely.

5 Beat together the soft cheese and icing (confectioners') sugar until combined. Beat in the melted chocolate. Split the cake in half and sandwich together again with half of the chocolate mixture. Cover the top of the cake with the remainder of the chocolate mixture, swirling it with a knife. Leave to chill or serve at once.

COOK'S TIP

The undecorated cake can be frozen for up to 2 months. Defrost at room temperature for 3 hours or overnight in the refrigerator.

Chocolate Yogurt Cake

*Adding yogurt to the cake mixture gives the baked
cake a deliciously moist texture.*

Serves 8-10

INGREDIENTS

150 ml/^{1}/$_4$ pint/^{2}/$_3$ cup vegetable oil
150 ml/^{1}/$_4$ pint/^{2}/$_3$ cup whole milk
   natural yogurt
175 g/6 oz/1^1/$_4$ cups light
   muscovado sugar
3 eggs, beaten
100 g/3^1/$_2$ oz/^{3}/$_4$ cup wholemeal
   (whole wheat) self-raising flour

125 g/4^1/$_2$ oz/1 cup self-raising flour,
   sieved (strained)
2 tbsp cocoa powder
1 tsp bicarbonate of soda (baking
   soda)
50 g/1^3/$_4$ oz dark chocolate, melted

FILLING AND TOPPING:
150 ml/^{1}/$_4$ pint/^{2}/$_3$ cup whole milk
   natural yogurt
150 ml/^{1}/$_4$ pint/^{2}/$_3$ cup double
   (heavy) cream
225 g/8 oz fresh soft fruit, such as
   strawberries or raspberries

1 Grease a deep 23 cm/9 inch round cake tin (pan) and line the base with baking parchment.

2 Place the oil, yogurt, sugar and beaten eggs in a large mixing bowl and beat together until well combined. Sieve (strain) the flours, cocoa powder and bicarbonate of soda (baking soda) together and beat into the bowl until well combined. Beat in the melted chocolate.

3 Pour into the prepared tin (pan) and bake in a preheated oven, 180°C/350°F/Gas Mark 4, for 45-50 minutes or until a fine skewer inserted into the centre comes out clean. Leave to cool in the tin (pan) for 5 minutes, then turn out on to a wire rack to cool completely. When cold, split the cake into 3 layers.

4 To make the filling, place the yogurt and cream in a large mixing bowl and whisk well until the mixture stands in soft peaks.

5 Place one layer of cake on to a serving plate and spread with some of the cream. Top with a little of the fruit (slicing larger fruit such as strawberries). Repeat with the next layer. Top with the final layer of cake and spread with the rest of the cream. Arrange more fruit on top and cut the cake into wedges to serve.

Chocolate Layer Log

This unusual cake is very popular with children who love the appearance of the layers when it is sliced.

Serves 8-10

INGREDIENTS

125 g/4¹/₂ oz/¹/₂ cup soft margarine
125 g/4¹/₂ oz/¹/₂ cup caster (superfine) sugar
2 eggs
100 g/3¹/₂ oz/³/₄ cup self-raising flour

25 g/1 oz/¹/₄ cup cocoa powder
2 tbsp milk

WHITE CHOCOLATE BUTTER CREAM:
75 g/2³/₄ oz white chocolate
2 tbsp milk

150 g/5¹/₂ oz/²/₃ cup butter
125 g/4¹/₂ oz/³/₄ cup icing (confectioners') sugar
2 tbsp orange-flavoured liqueur
large dark chocolate curls (see page 66), to decorate

1 Grease and line the sides of two 400 g/14 oz food cans.

2 Beat together the margarine and sugar in a bowl until light and fluffy. Gradually add the eggs, beating well after each addition. Sieve (strain) together the flour and cocoa powder and fold into the cake mixture. Fold in the milk.

3 Divide the mixture between the two prepared cans. Stand the cans on a baking tray (cookie sheet) and bake in a preheated oven, 180°C/350°F/Gas Mark 4, for 40 minutes or until springy to the touch. Leave to cool for about 5 minutes in the cans, then turn out and leave to cool completely on a wire rack.

4 To make the butter cream, put the chocolate and milk in a pan and heat gently until the chocolate has melted, stirring until well combined. Leave to cool slightly. Beat together the butter and icing (confectioners') sugar until light and fluffy. Beat in the orange liqueur. Gradually beat in the chocolate mixture.

5 To assemble, cut both cakes into 1 cm/¹/₂ inch thick slices, then reassemble them by sandwiching the slices together with some of the butter cream.

6 Place the cake on a serving plate and spread the remaining butter cream over the top and sides. Decorate with the chocolate curls, then serve the cake cut diagonally into slices.

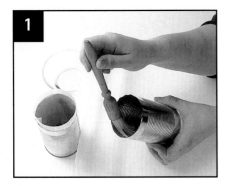

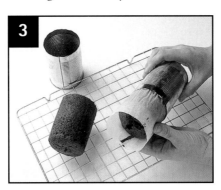

Chocolate & Orange Mousse Cake

With a dark chocolate sponge sandwiched together with a light creamy
orange mousse, this spectacular cake is irresistible.

Serves 12

INGREDIENTS

175 g/6 oz/^{3}/$_4$ cup butter
175 g/6 oz/^{3}/$_4$ cup caster (superfine)
 sugar
4 eggs, lightly beaten
200 g/7 oz/1^3/$_4$ cups self-raising
 flour
1 tbsp cocoa powder

50 g/1^3/$_4$ oz dark orange-flavoured
 chocolate, melted

ORANGE MOUSSE:
2 eggs, separated
50 g/1^3/$_4$ oz/4 tbsp caster (superfine)
 sugar

200 ml/7fl oz/^{3}/$_4$ cup freshly
 squeezed orange juice
2 tsp gelatine
3 tbsp water
300 ml/^{1}/$_2$ pint/1^1/$_4$ cups double
 (heavy) cream
peeled orange slices, to decorate

1 Grease a 20 cm/8 inch springform cake tin (pan) and and line the base. Beat the butter and sugar in a bowl until light and fluffy. Gradually add the eggs, beating well after each addition. Sieve (strain) together the cocoa and flour and fold into the cake mixture. Fold in the chocolate.

2 Pour into the prepared tin (pan) and level the top. Bake in a preheated oven, 180°C/350°F/ Gas Mark 4, for 40 minutes or

until springy to the touch. Leave to cool for 5 minutes in the tin (pan), then turn out and leave to cool completely on a wire rack. Cut the cold cake into 2 layers.

3 To make the orange mousse, beat the egg yolks and sugar until light, then whisk in the orange juice. Sprinkle the gelatine over the water in a small bowl and allow to go spongy, then place over a pan of hot water and stir until dissolved. Stir into the mousse.

4 Whip the cream until holding its shape, reserve a little for decoration and fold the rest into the mousse. Whisk the egg whites until standing in soft peaks, then fold in. Leave in a cool place until starting to set, stirring occasionally.

5 Place half of the cake in the tin (pan). Pour in the mousse and press the second cake layer on top. Chill until set. Transfer to a dish, pipe cream rosettes on the top and arrange orange slices in the centre.

Chocolate Roulade

Don't worry if the cake cracks when rolled, this is quite normal. If it doesn't crack, you can consider yourself a real chocolate wizard in the kitchen!

Serves 6-8

INGREDIENTS

150 g/5^1/2 oz dark chocolate
2 tbsp water
6 eggs
175 g/6 oz/^{3}/4 cup caster (superfine)
  sugar
25 g/1 oz/^{1}/4 cup plain (all-purpose)
  flour

1 tbsp cocoa powder

FILLING:
300 ml/^{1}/2 pint/1^1/4 cups double
  (heavy) cream
75 g/2^3/4 oz sliced strawberries

TO DECORATE:
icing (confectioners') sugar
chocolate leaves (see below)

1 Line a 37.5 × 25 cm/15 × 10 inch Swiss roll tin (pan). Melt the chocolate in the water, stirring. Leave to cool slightly.

2 Place the eggs and sugar in a bowl and whisk for 10 minutes, or until the mixture is pale and foamy and the whisk leaves a trail when lifted. Whisk in the chocolate in a thin stream. Sieve (strain) the flour and cocoa together and fold into the mixture. Pour into the tin; level the top.

3 Bake in a preheated oven, 200°C/400°F/Gas Mark 6, for 12 minutes. Dust a sheet of baking parchment with a little icing (confectioners') sugar. Turn out the roulade and remove the lining paper. Roll up the roulade with the fresh parchment inside. Place on a wire rack, cover with a damp tea towel and leave to cool.

4 Whisk the cream until just holding its shape. Unroll the roulade and scatter over the fruit.

Spread three-quarters of the cream over the roulade and re-roll. Dust with icing (confectioners') sugar. Place the roulade on a plate. Pipe the rest of the cream down the centre and decorate with chocolate leaves.

5 To make chocolate leaves, wash some rose or holly leaves and pat dry. Melt some chocolate and brush over the leaves. Set aside to harden. Repeat with 2-3 layers of chocolate. Carefully peel the leaves away from the chocolate.

Chocolate & Coconut Roulade

A coconut-flavoured roulade is encased in a rich chocolate coating. A fresh raspberry coulis gives a lovely fresh contrast to the sweetness of the roulade.

Serves 8–10

INGREDIENTS

3 eggs
75 g/2³/₄ oz/¹/₃ cup caster
    (superfine) sugar
50 g/1³/₄ oz/¹/₃ cup self-raising flour
1 tbsp block creamed coconut,
    softened with 1 tbsp boiling water

25 g/1 oz desiccated (shredded)
    coconut
6 tbsp good raspberry conserve

CHOCOLATE COATING:
200 g/7 oz dark chocolate
60 g/2 oz/¹/₄ cup butter

2 tbsp golden (light corn) syrup

RASPBERRY COULIS:
225 g/8 oz fresh or frozen
    raspberries, thawed if frozen
2 tbsp water
4 tbsp icing (confectioners') sugar

1 Grease and line a 23 × 30 cm/ 9 × 12 inch Swiss roll tin (pan). Whisk the eggs and caster (superfine) sugar in a large mixing bowl with electric beaters for about 10 minutes or until the mixture is very light and foamy and the whisk leaves a trail that lasts a few seconds when lifted.

2 Sieve (strain) the flour and fold in with a metal spoon or a spatula. Fold in the creamed coconut and desiccated (shredded) coconut. Pour into the prepared tin (pan) and bake in a preheated oven, 200°C/400°F/Gas Mark 6, for 10-12 minutes, or until springy to the touch.

3 Sprinkle a sheet of baking parchment with a little caster (superfine) sugar and place on top of a damp tea towel. Turn the cake out on to the paper and carefully peel away the lining paper. Spread the jam over the sponge and roll up from the short end, using the tea towel to help you. Place seam-side down on a wire rack and leave to cool completely.

4 To make the coating, melt the chocolate and butter, stirring. Stir in the golden (light corn) syrup; leave to cool for 5 minutes. Spread it over the roulade and leave to set. To make the coulis, purée the fruit in a food processor with the water and sugar; sieve to remove the seeds. Cut the roulade into slices and serve with the coulis.

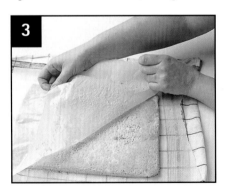

Almond & Hazelnut Gateau

This is a light nutty cake sandwiched together with a rich chocolate cream.
Simple to make, it is a gateau you are sure to make again and again.

Serves 8–10

INGREDIENTS

4 eggs
100 g/3^1/$_2$ oz/7 tbsp caster
    (superfine) sugar
50 g/1^3/$_4$ oz/^{1}/$_2$ cup ground almonds
50 g/1^3/$_4$ oz/^{1}/$_2$ cup ground
    hazelnuts

50 g/1^3/$_4$ oz/^{1}/$_3$ cup plain (all-
    purpose) flour
50 g/1^3/$_4$ oz/^{1}/$_2$ cup flaked almonds

FILLING:
100 g/3^1/$_2$ oz dark chocolate

15 g/^{1}/$_2$ oz/1 tbsp butter
300 ml/^{1}/$_2$ pint/1^1/$_4$ cups double
    (heavy) cream
icing (confectioners') sugar, to dust

1 Grease two 18 cm/7 inch round sandwich tins (pans) and line the bases with baking parchment.

2 Whisk the eggs and caster (superfine) sugar in a large mixing bowl with electric beaters for about 10 minutes, or until the mixture is very light and foamy and the whisk leaves a trail that lasts a few seconds when lifted.

3 Fold in the ground nuts, sieve (strain) the flour and fold in

with a metal spoon or spatula. Pour into the prepared tins (pans).

4 Scatter the flaked almonds over the top of one of the cakes. Bake both of the cakes in a preheated oven, 190°C/375°F/Gas Mark 5, for 15-20 minutes or until springy to the touch.

5 Leave the cakes to cool slightly in the tins (pans). Carefully remove the cakes from the tins (pans) and transfer them to a wire rack to cool completely.

6 To make the filling, melt the chocolate, remove from the heat and stir in the butter. Leave to cool slightly. Whip the cream until just holding its shape, then fold in the melted chocolate until mixed.

7 Place the cake without the extra almonds on a serving plate and spread the filling over it. Leave to set slightly, then place the almond-topped cake on top of the filling and leave to chill for about 1 hour. Dust with icing (confectioners') sugar and serve.

Chocolate & Walnut Cake

This walnut-studded chocolate cake has a tasty chocolate butter icing. It is perfect for serving at coffee mornings as it can easily be made the day before.

Serves 8-12

INGREDIENTS

4 eggs
125 g/4^1/$_2$ oz/^{1}/$_2$ cup caster
   (superfine) sugar
125 g/4^1/$_2$ oz/1 cup plain (all-
   purpose) flour
1 tbsp cocoa powder
25 g/1 oz/2 tbsp butter, melted

75 g/2^3/$_4$ oz dark chocolate, melted
150 g/5^1/$_2$ oz/1^1/$_4$ cups finely
   chopped walnuts

ICING:
75 g/2^3/$_4$ oz dark chocolate
125 g/4^1/$_2$ oz/^{1}/$_2$ cup butter

200 g/7 oz/1^1/$_4$ cups icing
   (confectioners') sugar
2 tbsp milk
walnut halves, to decorate

1 Grease a 18 cm/7 inch deep round cake tin (pan) and line the base. Place the eggs and caster (superfine) sugar in a mixing bowl and whisk with electric beaters for 10 minutes, or until the mixture is light and foamy and the whisk leaves a trail that lasts a few seconds when lifted.

2 Sieve (strain) together the flour and cocoa powder and fold in with a metal spoon or spatula. Fold in the melted butter

and chocolate, and the chopped walnuts. Pour into the prepared tin (pan) and bake in a preheated oven, 160°C/325°F/Gas Mark 3, and bake for 30-35 minutes or until springy to the touch.

3 Leave to cool in the tin (pan) for 5 minutes, then transfer to a wire rack to cool completely. Cut the cold cake into 2 layers.

4 To make the icing, melt the dark chocolate and leave to

cool slightly. Beat together the butter, icing (confectioners') sugar and milk in a bowl until the mixture is pale and fluffy. Whisk in the melted chocolate.

5 Sandwich the 2 cake layers with some of the icing and place on a serving plate. Spread the remaining icing over the top of the cake with a palette knife (spatula), swirling it slightly as you do so. Decorate the cake with the walnut halves and serve.

Dobos Torte

This wonderful cake originates from Hungary and consists of thin layers of light sponge sandwiched together with butter cream and topped with a crunchy caramel layer.

Serves 8

INGREDIENTS

3 eggs
100 g/3^1/$_2$ oz/7 tbsp caster (superfine) sugar
1 tsp vanilla flavouring (extract)
100 g/3^1/$_2$ oz/^{1}/$_2$ cup plain (all-purpose) flour

FILLING:
175 g/6 oz dark chocolate
175 g/6 oz/^{3}/$_4$ cup butter
2 tbsp milk
350 g/12 oz/2 cups icing (confectioners') sugar

CARAMEL:
100 g/3^1/$_2$ oz/7 tbsp granulated sugar
4 tbsp water

1 Draw four 18 cm/7 inch circles on sheets of baking parchment. Place 2 of them upside down on 2 baking trays (cookie sheets). Whisk the eggs and caster (superfine) sugar in a large mixing bowl with electric beaters for 10 minutes, or until the mixture is light and foamy and the whisk leaves a trail. Fold in the vanilla flavouring (extract). Sieve (strain) the flour and fold in with a metal spoon or a spatula. Spoon a quarter of the mixture on to one of the trays (sheets) and spread out to the size of the circle. Repeat with the other circle. Bake in a preheated oven, 200°C/400°F/Gas Mark 6, for 5-8 minutes or until golden brown. Cool on wire racks. Repeat with the remaining mixture.

2 To make the filling, melt the chocolate and cool slightly. Beat the butter, milk and icing (confectioners') sugar until pale and fluffy. Whisk in the chocolate. Place the sugar and water for the caramel in a heavy-based pan and heat gently, stirring until the sugar dissolves. Boil gently until the syrup is pale golden. Remove from the heat. Pour over one layer of the cake to cover the top. Leave to harden slightly, then mark into 8 portions with an oiled knife. Remove the cakes from the paper and trim the edges. Sandwich the layers together with some of the filling, finishing with the caramel-topped cake. Place on a serving plate and spread the sides with the filling mixture, using a comb scraper if you have one. Pipe rosettes around the top of the cake.

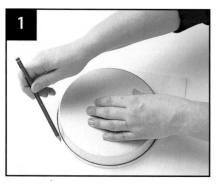

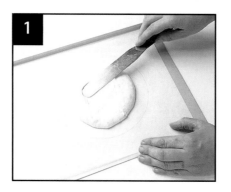

Bistvitny Torte

This is a Russian marbled chocolate cake that is soaked in a delicious flavoured syrup and decorated with chocolate and cream.

Serves 10

INGREDIENTS

CHOCOLATE TRIANGLES:
25 g/1 oz dark chocolate, melted
25 g/1 oz white chocolate, melted

CAKE:
175 g/6 oz/^{3}/$_4$ cup soft margarine

175 g/6 oz/^{3}/$_4$ cup caster (superfine) sugar
^{1}/$_2$ tsp vanilla flavouring (extract)
3 eggs, lightly beaten
225 g/8 oz/2 cups self-raising flour
50 g/1^3/$_4$ oz dark chocolate

SYRUP:
125 g/4^1/$_2$ oz/^{1}/$_2$ cup sugar
6 tbsp water
3 tbsp brandy or sherry
150 ml/^{1}/$_4$ pint/^{2}/$_3$ cup double (heavy) cream

1 Grease a 23 cm/9 inch ring tin (pan). To make the triangles, place a sheet of baking parchment on to a baking tray (cookie sheet) and place alternate spoonfuls of the dark and white chocolate on to the paper. Spread together to form a thick marbled layer; leave to set. Cut into squares, then into triangles.

2 To make the cake, beat the margarine and sugar until light and fluffy. Beat in the vanilla flavouring (extract). Gradually add the eggs, beating well after each addition. Fold in the flour. Divide the mixture in half. Melt the dark chocolate and stir into one half.

3 Place spoonfuls of each mixture into the prepared tin (pan) and swirl together with a skewer to create a marbled effect.

4 Bake in a preheated oven, 190°C/375°F/Gas Mark 5, for 30 minutes, or until the cake is springy to the touch. Leave to cool in the tin (pan) for a few minutes, then transfer to a wire rack to cool completely.

5 To make the syrup, place the sugar in a small pan with the water and heat until the sugar has dissolved. Boil for 1-2 minutes. Remove from the heat and stir in the brandy or sherry. Leave the syrup to cool slightly then spoon it slowly over the cake, allowing it to soak into the sponge. Whip the cream and pipe swirls of it on top of the cake. Decorate with the chocolate triangles.

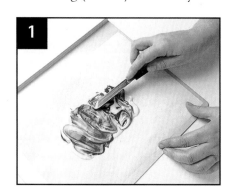

Sachertorte

This rich melt-in-the mouth cake originates in Austria. Make sure you have a steady hand when writing the name on the top. If preferred, you could drizzle a random scribble of chocolate instead.

Serves 10-12

INGREDIENTS

175 g/6 oz dark chocolate
150 g/5^1/$_2$ oz/^{2}/$_3$ cup unsalted butter
150 g/5^1/$_2$ oz/^{2}/$_3$ cup caster
   (superfine) sugar
6 eggs, separated

150 g/5^1/$_2$ oz/1^1/$_4$ cups plain (all-
  purpose) flour

ICING AND FILLING:
175 g/6 oz dark chocolate

5 tbsp strong black coffee
175 g/6 oz/1 cup icing
  (confectioners') sugar
6 tbsp good apricot preserve
50 g/1^3/$_4$ oz dark chocolate, melted

1 Grease a 23 cm/9 inch springform cake tin (pan) and line the base. Melt the chocolate. Beat the butter and 75 g/2^3/$_4$ oz/^{1}/$_3$ cup of the sugar until pale and fluffy. Add the egg yolks and beat well. Add the chocolate in a thin stream, beating well. Sieve (strain) the flour; fold it into the mixture. Whisk the egg whites until they stand in soft peaks. Add the remaining sugar and whisk for 2 minutes by hand, or 45-60 seconds if using an electric whisk, until glossy. Fold half into the chocolate mixture, then fold in the remainder.

2 Spoon into the prepared tin (pan) and level the top. Bake in a preheated oven, 150°C/300°F/ Gas Mark 2, for 1-1^1/$_4$ hours until a skewer inserted into the centre comes out clean. Cool in the tin (pan) for 5 minutes, then transfer to a wire rack to cool completely.

3 To make the icing, melt the chocolate and beat in the coffee until smooth. Sieve (strain) the icing (confectioners') sugar into a bowl. Whisk in the melted chocolate mixture to give a thick icing. Halve the cake. Warm the

jam, spread over one half of the cake and sandwich together. Invert the cake on a wire rack. Spoon the icing over the cake and spread to coat the top and sides. Leave to set for 5 minutes, allowing any excess icing to drop through the rack. Transfer to a serving plate and leave to set for at least 2 hours.

4 To decorate, spoon the melted chocolate into a small piping bag and pipe the word 'Sacher' or 'Sachertorte' on the top of the cake. Leave it to harden before serving the cake.

Dark & White Chocolate Torte

*If you can't decide if you prefer bitter dark chocolate or rich creamy
white chocolate then this gateau is for you.*

Serves 10

INGREDIENTS

4 eggs
100 g/3^1/$_2$ oz/7 tbsp cup caster
   (superfine) sugar
100 g/3^1/$_2$ oz/^{3}/$_4$ cup plain (all-
   purpose) flour

DARK CHOCOLATE CREAM:
300 ml/^{1}/$_2$ pint/^{2}/$_3$ cup double
   (heavy) cream
150 g/5^1/$_2$ oz dark chocolate, broken
   into small pieces

WHITE CHOCOLATE ICING:
75 g/2^3/$_4$ oz white chocolate
15 g/^{1}/$_2$ oz/1 tbsp butter
1 tbsp milk
50 g/1^3/$_4$ oz/4 tbsp icing
   (confectioners') sugar
chocolate caraque (see page 208)

1 Grease a 20 cm/8 inch round springform tin (pan) and line the base. Whisk the eggs and caster (superfine) sugar in a large mixing bowl with electric beaters for about 10 minutes, or until the mixture is very light and foamy and the whisk leaves a trail that lasts a few seconds when lifted.

2 Sieve (strain) the flour and fold in with a metal spoon or spatula. Pour into the prepared tin (pan) and bake in a preheated oven, 180°C/350°F/Gas Mark 4, for 35-40 minutes, or until springy to the touch. Leave to cool slightly, then transfer to a wire rack to cool completely. Cut the cold cake into 2 layers.

3 To make the chocolate cream, place the cream in a saucepan and bring to the boil, stirring. Add the chocolate and stir until melted and well combined. Remove from the heat and leave to cool. Beat with a wooden spoon until thick.

4 Sandwich the 2 cake layers back together with the chocolate cream and place on a wire rack.

5 To make the icing, melt the chocolate and butter together and stir until blended. Whisk in the milk and icing (confectioners') sugar. Whisk for a few minutes until the icing is cool. Pour it over the cake and spread with a palette knife (spatula) to coat the top and sides. Decorate with chocolate caraque and leave to set.

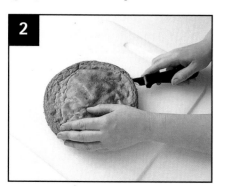

Chocolate Ganache Cake

Ganache – a divine mixture of chocolate and cream – is used to fill and decorate this rich chocolate cake, making it a chocolate lover's dream.

Serves 10-12

INGREDIENTS

175 g/6 oz/^{3}/4 cup butter
175 g/6 oz/^{3}/4 cup caster (superfine) sugar
4 eggs, lightly beaten
200 g/7 oz/1^3/4 cups self-raising flour

1 tbsp cocoa powder
50 g/1^3/4 oz dark chocolate, melted

GANACHE:
450ml/16 fl oz/2 cups double (heavy) cream

375 g/13 oz dark chocolate, broken into pieces

TO FINISH:
200 g/7 oz chocolate-flavoured cake covering

1 Lightly grease a 20 cm/8 inch springform cake tin (pan) and line the base. Beat the butter and sugar until light and fluffy. Gradually add the eggs, beating well after each addition. Sieve (strain) together the flour and cocoa. Fold into the cake mixture. Fold in the melted chocolate.

2 Pour into the prepared tin (pan) and level the top. Bake in a preheated oven, 180°C/350°F/ Gas Mark 4, for 40 minutes or until springy to the touch. Leave to cool for 5 minutes in the tin (pan), then turn out on to a wire rack and leave to cool completely . Cut the cold cake into 2 layers.

3 To make the ganache, place the cream in a pan and bring to the boil, stirring. Add the chocolate and stir until melted and combined. Pour into a bowl and whisk for about 5 minutes or until the ganache is fluffy and cool.

4 Reserve one-third of the ganache. Use the remaining ganache to sandwich the cake together and spread over the top and sides of the cake.

5 Melt the cake covering and spread it over a large sheet of baking parchment. Cool until just set. Cut into strips a little wider than the height of the cake. Place the strips around the edge of the cake, overlapping them slightly.

6 Pipe the reserved ganache in tear drop or shells to cover the top of the cake. Chill for 1 hour.

Bûche de Noël

This is the traditional French Christmas cake. It consists of a chocolate Swiss roll filled and encased in a delicious rich chocolate icing.

Serves 8–10

INGREDIENTS

CAKE:
4 eggs
100 g/3^1/2 oz/7 tbsp caster
   (superfine) sugar
75 g/2^3/4 oz/^{2}/3 cup self-raising flour
2 tbsp cocoa powder

ICING:
150 g/5^1/2 oz dark chocolate
2 egg yolks
150 ml/^{1}/4 pint/^{2}/3 cup milk
125 g/4^1/2 oz/^{1}/2 cup butter
50 g/1^3/4 oz/4 tbsp icing
   (confectioners') sugar

2 tbsp rum (optional)

TO DECORATE:
a little white glacé or royal icing
icing (confectioners') sugar, to dust
holly or Christmas cake decorations

1 Grease and line a 30 × 23 cm/ 12 × 9 inch Swiss roll tin (pan). Whisk the eggs and caster (superfine) sugar in a bowl with electric beaters for 10 minutes, or until the mixture is very light and foamy and the whisk leaves a trail. Sieve (strain) the flour and cocoa powder and fold in. Pour into the prepared tin (pan) and bake in a preheated oven, 200°C/400°F/Gas Mark 6, for 12 minutes or until springy to the touch. Turn out on to a piece of baking parchment which has been sprinkled with a little caster (superfine) sugar. Peel off the lining paper and trim the edges. Cut a small slit halfway into the cake about 1 cm/^{1}/2 inch from one short end. Starting at that end, roll up tightly, enclosing the paper. Place on a wire rack to cool.

2 To make the icing, break the chocolate into pieces and melt it over a pan of hot water. Beat in the egg yolks, whisk in the milk and cook until the mixture thickens enough to coat the back of a wooden spoon, stirring. Cover with dampened greaseproof paper and cool. Beat the butter and sugar until pale and fluffy. Beat in the custard and rum, if using. Unroll the sponge, spread with one-third of the icing and roll up again. Place on a serving plate. Spread the remaining icing over the cake and mark with a fork to give the effect of bark. Leave to set. Pipe white icing to form the rings of the log. Sprinkle with sugar and decorate.

Chocolate Truffle Cake

*Soft chocolatey sponge topped with a rich chocolate truffle mixture
makes a cake that chocoholics will die for.*

Serves 12

INGREDIENTS

75 g/2³/₄ oz/¹/₃ cup butter
75 g/2³/₄ oz/¹/₃ cup caster
  (superfine) sugar
2 eggs, lightly beaten
75 g/2³/₄ oz/²/₃ cup self-raising flour
¹/₂ tsp baking powder
25 g/1 oz/¹/₄ cup cocoa powder
50 g/1³/₄ oz ground almonds

TRUFFLE TOPPING:
350 g/12 oz dark chocolate
100 g/3¹/₂ oz butter
300 ml/¹/₂ pint/1¹/₄ cups double
  (heavy) cream
75 g/2³/₄ oz/1¹/₄ cups plain cake
  crumbs
3 tbsp dark rum

TO DECORATE:
Cape gooseberries
50 g/1³/₄ oz dark chocolate, melted

1 Lightly grease a 20 cm/8 inch round springform tin (pan) and line the base. Beat together the butter and sugar until light and fluffy. Gradually add the eggs, beating well after each addition.

2 Sieve (strain) the flour, baking powder and cocoa powder together and fold into the mixture along with the ground almonds. Pour into the prepared tin (pan) and bake in a preheated oven, 180°C/350°F/Gas Mark 4, for 20-25 minutes or until springy to the touch. Leave to cool slightly in the tin (pan), then transfer to a wire rack to cool completely. Wash and dry the tin (pan) and return the cooled cake to the tin (pan).

3 To make the topping, heat the chocolate, butter and cream in a heavy-based pan over a low heat and stir until smooth. Cool, then chill for 30 minutes. Beat well with a wooden spoon and chill for a further 30 minutes. Beat the mixture again, then add the cake crumbs and rum, beating until well combined. Spoon over the sponge base and chill for 3 hours.

4 Meanwhile, dip the Cape gooseberries in the melted chocolate until partially covered. Leave to set on baking parchment. Transfer the cake to a serving plate; decorate with Cape gooseberries.

White Chocolate Truffle Cake

A light white sponge, topped with a rich creamy-white chocolate truffle mixture makes an out-of-this-world gateau.

Serves 12

INGREDIENTS

2 eggs
50 g/1³/4 oz/4 tbsp caster (superfine) sugar
50 g/1³/4 oz/¹/3 cup plain (all-purpose) flour
50 g/1³/4 oz white chocolate, melted

TRUFFLE TOPPIING:
300 ml/¹/2 pint/1¹/4 cups double (heavy) cream
350 g/12 oz white chocolate, broken into pieces
250 g/9 oz Quark or fromage frais

TO DECORATE:
dark, milk or white chocolate, melted
cocoa powder, to dust

1 Grease a 20 cm/8 inch round springform tin (pan) and line the base. Whisk the eggs and caster (superfine) sugar in a mixing bowl for 10 minutes, or until the mixture is very light and foamy and the whisk leaves a trail that lasts a few seconds when lifted. Sieve (strain) the flour and fold in with a metal spoon. Fold in the melted white chocolate. Pour into the tin (pan) and bake in a preheated oven, 180°C/350°F/Gas Mark 4, for 25 minutes or until springy to the touch. Leave to cool slightly, then transfer to a wire rack until completely cold. Return the cold cake to the tin (pan).

2 To make the topping, place the cream in a pan and bring to the boil, stirring to prevent it sticking to the bottom of the pan. Cool slightly, then add the white chocolate pieces and stir until melted and combined. Remove from the heat and leave until almost cool, stirring, then stir in the Quark or fromage frais. Pour the mixture on top of the cake and chill for 2 hours. Remove the cake from the tin (pan) and transfer to a serving plate.

3 To make large chocolate curls, pour melted chocolate on to a marble or acrylic board and spread it thinly with a palette knife (spatula). Leave to set at room temperature. Using a scraper, push through the chocolate at a 25° angle until a large curl forms. Remove each curl as you make it and leave to chill until set. Decorate the cake with chocolate curls and sprinkle with a little cocoa powder.

Chocolate & Raspberry Vacherin

A vacherin is made of layers of crisp meringue sandwiched together with fruit and cream. It makes a fabulous gateau for special occasions.

Serves 10–12

INGREDIENTS

3 egg whites
175 g/6 oz/³/4 cup caster (superfine) sugar
1 tsp cornflour (cornstarch)
25 g/1 oz dark chocolate, grated

FILLING:
175 g/6 oz dark chocolate
450 ml/16 fl oz/2 cups double (heavy) cream, whipped

350 g/12 oz fresh raspberries
a little melted chocolate, to decorate

1 Draw 3 rectangles, 10 × 25 cm/ 4 × 10 inches, on sheets of baking parchment and place on 2 baking trays (cookie sheets).

2 Whisk the egg whites in a mixing bowl until standing in soft peaks, then gradually whisk in half of the sugar and continue whisking until the mixture is very stiff and glossy.

3 Carefully fold in the rest of the sugar, the cornflour (cornstarch) and grated chocolate with a metal spoon or a spatula.

4 Spoon the meringue mixture into a piping bag fitted with a 1 cm/¹/2 inch plain nozzle (tip) and pipe lines across the rectangles.

5 Bake in a preheated oven, 140°C/275°F/Gas Mark 1, for 1¹/2 hours, changing the positions of the baking trays (cookie sheets) halfway through. Without opening the oven door, turn off the oven and leave the meringues to cool in the oven, then peel away the paper.

6 To make the filling, melt the chocolate and spread it over

2 of the meringue layers. Leave the filling to harden.

7 Place 1 chocolate-coated meringue on a plate and top with about one-third of the cream and raspberries. Gently place the second chocolate-coated meringue on top and spread with half of the remaining cream and raspberries.

8 Place the last meringue on the top and decorate it with the remaining cream and raspberries. Drizzle a little melted chocolate over the top and serve.

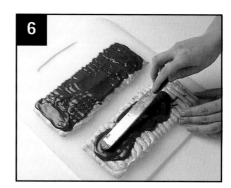

Tropical Fruit Vacherin

Meringue layers are sandwiched with a rich chocolate cream and topped with tropical fruit. Prepare in advance and make up just before required.

Serves 10–12

INGREDIENTS

6 egg whites
275 g/9¹/₂ oz/generous 1 cup caster (superfine) sugar
75 g/2³/₄ oz/³/₄ cup desiccated (shredded) coconut

FILLING AND TOPPING:
90 g/3 oz dark chocolate, broken into pieces
3 egg yolks
3 tbsp water
1 tbsp rum (optional)

50 g/1³/₄ oz/4 tbsp caster (superfine) sugar
450 ml/16 fl oz/2 cups double (heavy) cream
selection of tropical fruits, sliced or cut into bite size pieces

1 Draw 3 circles, 20 cm/8 inch each, on sheets of baking parchment and place on baking trays (cookie sheets).

2 Whisk the egg whites until standing in soft peaks, then gradually whisk in half of the sugar and continue whisking until the mixture is very stiff and glossy. Carefully fold in the remaining sugar and the coconut.

3 Spoon the mixture into a piping bag fitted with a star nozzle (tip) and cover the circles with piped swirls. Bake in a preheated oven, 140°C/275°F/Gas Mark 1, for 1¹/₂ hours, changing the position of the trays (sheets) halfway through. Without opening the oven door, turn off the oven and leave the meringues to cool in the oven, then peel away the paper.

4 To make the filling, place the chocolate pieces, egg yolks, water, rum, if using, and sugar in a small bowl and place it over a pan of gently simmering water. Cook over a low heat, stirring, until the chocolate has melted and the mixture has thickened. Cover with a disc of baking parchment and leave until cold.

5 Whip the cream and fold two-thirds of it into the chocolate mixture. Sandwich the meringue layers together with the chocolate mixture. Place the remaining cream in a piping bag fitted with a star nozzle (tip) and pipe around the edge of the meringue. Arrange the tropical fruits in the centre.

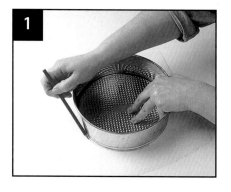

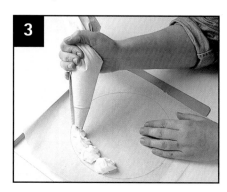

Small Cakes & Cookies

This chapter contains everyday delights for chocolate fans. You are sure to be tempted by our wonderful array of cookies and small cakes. Make any day special with a home-made chocolate biscuit (cookie) to be served with coffee, as a snack or to accompany a special dessert. Although some take a little longer to make, most are quick and easy to prepare and decoration is often simple although you can get carried away if you like!

You'll find recipes for old favourites such as Chocolate Chip Muffins and Chocolate Chip Cookies, Chocolate Butterfly Cakes and Sticky Chocolate Brownies. There are also some new biscuits (cookies) and small cakes to tickle your taste-buds, try Chocolate & Coconut Squares or Malted Chocolate Wedges. Finally, we have given the chocolate treatment to some traditional recipes, turning them into chocoholics delights – try Chocolate Scones or Chocolate Chip Flapjacks.

Chocolate Boxes

People will think you have spent hours in the kitchen producing theses delectable chocolate boxes, but with a few tricks (such as using ready-made cake) you can make them in no time at all.

Makes 4

INGREDIENTS

225 g/8 oz dark chocolate
about 225 g/8 oz bought or ready-
   made plain or chocolate cake
2 tbsp apricot jam

150 ml/¹/₄ pint/²/₃ cup double
   (heavy) cream
1 tbsp maple syrup

100 g/3¹/₂.oz prepared fresh fruit,
   such as small strawberries,
   raspberries, kiwi fruit or
   redcurrants

1 Melt the dark chocolate and spread it evenly over a large sheet of baking parchment. Leave to harden in a cool room.

2 When just set, cut the chocolate into 5 cm/2 inch squares and remove from the paper. Make sure that your hands are as cool as possible and handle the chocolate as little as possible.

3 Cut the cake into two 5 cm/ 2 inch cubes, then each cube in half. Warm the apricot jam and brush it over the sides of the cake cubes. Carefully press a chocolate

square on to each side of the cake cubes to give 4 chocolate boxes with cake at the bottom. Leave to chill for 20 minutes.

4 Whip the double (heavy) cream with the maple syrup until just holding its shape. Spoon or pipe a little of the mixture into each chocolate box.

5 Decorate the top of each box with the prepared fruit. If liked, the fruit can be partially dipped into melted chocolate and allowed to harden before putting into the boxes.

COOK'S TIP

For the best results, keep the boxes well chilled and fill and decorate them just before you want to serve them.

Chocolate Dairy Wraps

Light chocolate sponge is wrapped around a dairy cream filling.
These individual cakes can be served for dessert, if liked.

Makes 6–8

INGREDIENTS

2 eggs
50 g/1³/₄ oz/4 tbsp caster (superfine)
   sugar

50 g/1³/₄ oz/¹/₃ cup plain (all-
   purpose) flour
1¹/₂ tbsp cocoa powder
4 tbsp apricot jam

150 ml/¹/₄ pint/²/₃ cup double
   (heavy) cream, whipped
icing (confectioners') sugar, to dust

1 Line 2 baking trays (cookie sheets) with pieces of baking parchment. Whisk the eggs and sugar together until the mixture is very light and fluffy and the whisk leaves a trail when lifted.

2 Sift together the flour and cocoa powder. Using a metal spoon or a spatula, gently fold it into the eggs and sugar in a figure of eight movement.

3 Drop rounded tablespoons of the mixture on to the lined baking trays (cookie sheets) and spread them into oval shapes.

Make sure they are well spaced as they will spread during cooking.

4 Bake in a preheated oven, 220°C/425°F/Gas Mark 7, for about 6-8 minutes or until springy to the touch. Leave to cool on the baking trays (cookie sheets).

5 When cold, slide the cakes on to a damp tea towel and allow to stand until cold. Carefully remove them from the dampened paper. Spread the flat side of the cakes with jam, then spoon or pipe the whipped cream down the centre of each one.

6 Fold the cakes in half and place them on a serving plate. Sprinkle them with a little icing (confectioners') sugar and serve.

VARIATION

Fold 4 tsp of crème de menthe or 50 g/2 oz melted chocolate into the cream for fabulous alternatives to plain dairy cream.

Chocolate Cup Cakes with White Chocolate Icing

A variation on an old favourite, both kids and grown-ups will love these sumptuous little cakes.

Makes 18

INGREDIENTS

100 g/3¹/₂ oz/ generous ¹/₃ cup
   butter, softened
100 g/3¹/₂ oz/7 tbsp caster
   (superfine) sugar
2 eggs, lightly beaten

50 g/1³/₄ oz/¹/₃ cup dark chocolate
   chips
2 tbsp milk
150 g/5¹/₂ oz/1¹/₄ cups self-raising
   flour

25 g/1 oz/¹/₄ cup cocoa powder

ICING:
225 g/8 oz white chocolate
150 g/5¹/₂ oz low-fat soft cheese

1 Line an 18 hole bun tray with individual paper cup cases.

2 Beat together the butter and sugar until pale and fluffy. Gradually add the eggs, beating well after each addition. Add a little of the flour if the mixture begins to curdle. Add the milk, then fold in the chocolate chips.

3 Sift together the flour and cocoa powder and fold into the mixture with a metal spoon or spatula. Divide the mixture equally between the paper cases and level the tops.

4 Bake in a preheated oven, 180°C/350°F/Gas Mark 4, for 20 minutes, or until well risen and springy to the touch. Leave to cool on a wire rack.

5 To make the icing, melt the chocolate, then leave to cool slightly. Beat the cream cheese until softened slightly, then beat in the melted chocolate. Spread a little of the icing over each cake and chill for 1 hour before serving.

VARIATION

Add white chocolate chips or chopped pecan nuts to the mixture instead of the dark chocolate chips, if you prefer. You can also add the finely grated rind of 1 orange for a chocolate and orange flavour.

Chocolate Rum Babas

A little bit fiddly to make but well worth the effort. Indulge in these tasty cakes with coffee.
Or if like me you want to serve these as a dessert, serve them with soft summer fruits.

Makes 4

INGREDIENTS

100 g/3^{1}/$_{2}$ oz/^{3}/$_{4}$ cup strong plain
   (all-purpose) flour
25 g/1 oz/^{1}/$_{4}$ cup cocoa powder
6 g sachet easy blend yeast
pinch of salt
15 g/^{1}/$_{2}$ oz/1 tbsp caster (superfine)
   sugar

40 g/1^{1}/$_{2}$ oz dark chocolate, grated
2 eggs
3 tbsp tepid milk
50 g/1^{3}/$_{4}$ oz/4 tbsp butter, melted

SYRUP:
4 tbsp clear honey

2 tbsp water
4 tbsp rum

TO SERVE:
whipped cream
cocoa powder, to dust
fresh fruit (optional)

1 Lightly oil 4 individual ring tins (pans). In a large warmed mixing bowl, sieve (strain) the flour and cocoa powder together. Stir in the yeast, salt, sugar and grated chocolate. Beat the eggs together, add the milk and butter and beat until mixed.

2 Make a well in the centre of the dry ingredients and pour in the egg mixture, beating to mix to a batter. Beat for 10 minutes, ideally in a electric mixer with a dough hook. Divide the mixture between the tins (pans) – it should come halfway up the sides.

3 Place on a baking tray (cookie sheet) and cover with a damp tea towel. Leave in a warm place until the mixture rises almost to the tops of the tins (pans).Bake in a preheated oven, 200°C/400°F/ Gas Mark 6, for 15 minutes.

4 To make the syrup, gently heat all of the ingredients in a small pan. Turn out the babas and place on rack placed above a tray to catch the syrup. Drizzle the syrup over the babas and leave for at least 2 hours for the syrup to soak in. Once or twice, spoon the syrup that has dripped on to the tray over the babas.

5 Fill the centre of the babas with whipped cream and sprinkle a little cocoa powder over the top. Serve the babas with fresh fruit, if desired.

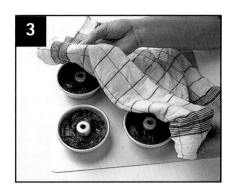

No Bake Chocolate Squares

These are handy little squares to keep in the refrigerator for when unexpected guests arrive.
Children will enjoy making these as an introduction to chocolate cookery.

Makes 16

INGREDIENTS

275 g/9^1/$_2$ oz dark chocolate
175 g/6 oz/^{3}/$_4$ cup butter
4 tbsp golden (light corn) syrup
2 tbsp dark rum (optional)

175 g/6 oz plain biscuits (cookies),
   such as Rich Tea
25 g/1 oz toasted rice cereal
50 g/1^3/$_4$ oz/^{1}/$_2$ cup chopped walnuts
   or pecan nuts

100 g/3^1/$_2$ oz/^{1}/$_2$ cup glacé (candied)
   cherries, chopped roughly
25 g/1 oz white chocolate, to
   decorate

1 Place the dark chocolate in a large mixing bowl with the butter, syrup and rum, if using, and set over a saucepan of gently simmering water until melted, stirring until blended.

2 Break the biscuits (cookies) into small pieces and stir into the chocolate mixture along with the rice cereal, nuts and cherries.

3 Line an 18 cm/7inch square cake tin (pan) with baking parchment. Pour the mixture into the tin (pan) and level the top,

pressing down well with the back of a spoon. Chill for 2 hours.

4 To decorate, melt the white chocolate and drizzle it over the top of the cake in a random pattern. Leave to set. To serve, carefully turn out of the tin (pan) and remove the baking parchment. Cut into 16 squares.

COOK'S TIP

Store in an airtight container in the refrigerator for up to 2 weeks.

VARIATION

Brandy or an orange-flavoured liqueur can be used instead of the rum, if you prefer. Cherry brandy also works well.

VARIATION

For a coconut flavour, replace the rice cereal with desiccated (shredded) coconut and add a coconut-flavoured liqueur.

Chocolate Butterfly Cakes

*Filled with a tangy lemon cream these appealing cakes
will be a favourite with adults and children alike.*

Makes 12

INGREDIENTS

125 g/4^1/$_2$ oz/^{1}/$_2$ cup soft margarine
125 g/4^1/$_2$ oz/^{1}/$_2$ cup caster
 (superfine) sugar
150 g/5^1/$_2$ oz/1^1/$_4$ cups self-raising
 flour
2 large eggs
2 tbsp cocoa powder

25 g/1 oz dark chocolate,
 melted

LEMON BUTTER CREAM:
100 g/3^1/$_2$ oz/ generous ^{1}/$_3$ cup
 unsalted butter, softened

225 g/8 oz/1^1/$_3$ cups icing
 (confectioners') sugar, sieved
 (strained)
grated rind of ^{1}/$_2$ lemon
1 tbsp lemon juice
icing (confectioners') sugar, to dust

1 Place 12 paper cases in a bun tray (sheet). Place all of the ingredients for the cakes, except for the melted chocolate, in a large mixing bowl and beat with electric beaters until the mixture is just smooth. Beat in the chocolate.

2 Spoon equal amounts of the cake mixture into each paper case, filling them three-quarters full. Bake in a preheated oven, 180°C/350°F/Gas Mark 4, for 15 minutes or until springy to the

touch. Transfer the cakes to a wire rack and leave to cool.

3 To make the lemon butter cream, place the butter in a mixing bowl and beat until fluffy, then gradually beat in the icing (confectioners') sugar. Beat in the lemon rind and gradually add the lemon juice, beating well.

4 When cold, cut the top off each cake, using a serrated knife. Cut each top in half.

5 Spread or pipe the butter cream icing over the cut surface of each cake and push the 2 cut pieces of cake top into the icing to form wings. Sprinkle with icing (confectioners') sugar.

VARIATION

For a chocolate butter cream, beat the butter and icing (confectioners') sugar together, then beat in 25 g/ 1 oz melted dark chocolate.

Sticky Chocolate Brownies

Everyone loves chocolate brownies and these are so gooey and delicious they are impossible to resist!

Makes 9

INGREDIENTS

100 g/3^1/$_2$ oz/generous ^{1}/$_3$ cup
  unsalted butter
175 g/6 oz/^{3}/$_4$ cup caster (superfine)
  sugar
75 g/2 ^{3}/$_4$ oz/^{1}/$_2$ cup dark muscovado
  sugar

125 g/4^1/$_2$ oz dark chocolate
1 tbsp golden (light corn) syrup
2 eggs
1 tsp chocolate or vanilla flavouring
  (extract)

100 g/3^1/$_2$ oz/^{3}/$_4$ cup plain (all-
  purpose) flour
2 tbsp cocoa powder
^{1}/$_2$ tsp baking powder

1 Lightly grease a 20 cm/8 inch shallow square cake tin (pan) and line the base.

2 Place the butter, sugars, dark chocolate and golden (light corn) syrup in a heavy-based saucepan and heat gently, stirring until the mixture is well blended and smooth. Remove from the heat and leave to cool.

3 Beat together the eggs and flavouring (extract). Whisk in the cooled chocolate mixture.

4 Sieve (strain) together the flour, cocoa powder and baking powder and fold carefully into the egg and chocolate mixture, using a metal spoon or a spatula.

5 Spoon the mixture into the prepared tin (pan) and bake in a preheated oven, 180°C/350°F/ Gas Mark 4, for 25 minutes until the top is crisp and the edge of the cake is beginning to shrink away from the tin (pan). The inside of the cake mixture will still be quite stodgy and soft to the touch.

6 Leave the cake to cool completely in the tin (pan), then cut it into squares to serve.

COOK'S TIP

This cake can be well wrapped and frozen for up to 2 months. Defrost at room temperature for about 2 hours or overnight in the refrigerator.

Chocolate Fudge Brownies

Chocolate brownies are very popular, here a traditional brownie mixture has a cream cheese ribbon through the centre and is topped with a delicious chocolate fudge icing.

Makes 16

INGREDIENTS

200 g/7 oz low-fat soft cheese
$^1/_2$ tsp vanilla flavouring (extract)
2 eggs
250 g/9 oz/generous 1 cup caster (superfine) sugar
100 g/3$^1/_2$ oz/generous $^1/_3$ cup butter
3 tbsp cocoa powder

100 g/3$^1/_2$ oz/$^3/_4$ cup self-raising flour, sieved (strained)
50 g/1$^3/_4$ oz pecans, chopped

FUDGE ICING:
50 g/1$^3/_4$ oz/1 tbsp butter
1 tbsp milk

100 g/3$^1/_2$ oz/$^1/_2$ cup icing (confectioners') sugar
2 tbsp cocoa powder
pecans, to decorate (optional)

1 Lightly grease a 20 cm/8 inch square shallow cake tin (pan) and line the base.

2 Beat together the cheese, vanilla flavouring (extract) and 25 g/1 oz/5 tsp of the caster (superfine) sugar until smooth, then set aside.

3 Beat the eggs and remaining caster (superfine) sugar together until light and fluffy. Place the butter and cocoa powder in a small pan and heat gently, stirring until the butter melts and the mixture combines, then stir it into the egg mixture. Fold in the flour and nuts.

4 Pour half of the brownie mixture into the tin (pan) and level the top. Carefully spread the soft cheese over it, then cover it with the remaining brownie mixture. Bake in a preheated oven, 180°C/350°F/Gas Mark 4, for 40-45 minutes. Cool in the tin (pan).

5 To make the icing, melt the butter in the milk. Stir in the icing (confectioners') sugar and cocoa powder. Spread the icing over the brownies and decorate with pecan nuts, if using. Leave the icing to set, then cut into squares to serve.

VARIATION

Omit the cheese layer if preferred. Use walnuts in place of the pecans.

Chocolate Chip Muffins

Muffins are always popular and are so simple to make. I make mini muffins for my young children which are fabulous bite-size treats or perfect for children parties.

Makes 12

INGREDIENTS

100 g/3^1/$_2$ oz/generous ^{1}/$_3$ cup soft margarine

225 g/8 oz/1 cup caster (superfine) sugar

2 large eggs

150 ml/^{1}/$_4$ pint/^{2}/$_3$ cup whole milk natural yogurt

5 tbsp milk

275 g/9^1/$_2$ oz/2 cups plain (all-purpose) flour

1 tsp bicarbonate of soda (baking soda)

175 g/6 oz dark chocolate chips

1 Line 12 muffin tins (pans) with paper cases.

2 Place the margarine and sugar in a large mixing bowl and beat with a wooden spoon until light and fluffy. Beat in the eggs, yogurt and milk until combined.

3 Sieve (strain) the flour and bicarbonate of soda (baking soda) together and add to the mixture. Stir until just blended.

4 Stir in the chocolate chips, then spoon the mixture into the paper cases and bake in a preheated oven, 190°C/375°F/Gas Mark 5, for 25 minutes or until a fine skewer inserted into the centre comes out clean. Leave to cool in the tin (pan) for 5 minutes, then turn out on to a wire rack to cool completely.

VARIATION

The mixture can also be used to make 6 large or 24 mini muffins. Bake mini muffins for 10 minutes or until springy to the touch.

VARIATION

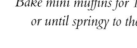

For chocolate and orange muffins, add the grated rind of 1 orange and replace the milk with fresh orange juice.

Chocolate Scones

*A plain scone mixture is transformed into a chocoholics treat
by the simple addition of chocolate chips.*

Makes 9

INGREDIENTS

225 g/8 oz/2 cups self-raising flour,
sieved (strained)

60 g/2 oz/¹/4 cup butter
1 tbsp caster (superfine) sugar

50 g/1³/4 oz/¹/3 cup chocolate chips
about 150 ml/¹/4 pint/²/3 cup milk

1 Lightly grease a baking tray (cookie sheet). Place the flour in a mixing bowl. Cut the butter into small pieces and rub it into the flour with your fingertips until the scone mixture resembles fine breadcrumbs.

2 Stir in the caster (superfine) sugar and chocolate chips.

3 Mix in enough milk to form a soft dough.

4 On a lightly floured surface, roll out the dough to form a rectangle 10 × 15 cm/4 × 6 inches, about 2.5 cm/1 inch thick. Cut the dough into 9 squares.

5 Place the scones spaced well apart on the prepared baking tray (cookie sheet).

6 Brush with a little milk and bake in a preheated oven, 220°C/425°F/Gas Mark 7, for 10-12 minutes until the scones are risen and golden.

COOK'S TIP

To be at their best, all scones should be freshly baked and served warm. Split the warm scones and spread them with a little chocolate and hazelnut spread or a good dollop of whipped cream.

VARIATION

Use dark, milk or white chocolate chips or a mixture of all three. Use a 5 cm/2 inch biscuit (cookie) cutter to cut out round scones, if preferred.

Pain au Chocolate

These croissants can be a little fiddly to make, but when you taste the light flaky layers of pastry enclosing a fabulous rich chocolate filling you know they are worth the effort.

Makes 12

INGREDIENTS

450 g/1 lb/4 cups strong plain (all-purpose) flour
^{1}/$_2$ tsp salt
6 g sachet of easy blend yeast
25 g/1 oz/2 tbsp white vegetable fat

1 egg, beaten lightly
225 ml/8 fl oz/1 cup tepid water
175 g/6 oz/^{3}/$_4$ cup butter, softened
100 g/3^1/$_2$ oz dark chocolate, broken into 12 squares

beaten egg, to glaze
icing (confectioners') sugar, to dust

1 Lightly grease a baking tray (cookie sheet). Sieve (strain) the flour and salt into a mixing bowl and stir in the yeast. Rub in the fat with your fingertips. Add the egg and enough of the water to mix to a soft dough. Knead it for about 10 minutes to make a smooth elastic dough.

2 Roll out to form a rectangle 37.5 × 20 cm/15 × 8 inches. Divide the butter into 3 portions and dot one portion over two-thirds of the rectangle, leaving a small border around the edge.

3 Fold the rectangle into 3 by first folding the plain part of the dough over and then the other side. Seal the edges of the dough by pressing with a rolling pin. Give the dough a quarter turn so the sealed edges are at the top and bottom. Re-roll and fold (without adding butter), then wrap the dough and chill for 30 minutes.

4 Repeat steps 2 and 3 until all of the butter has been used, chilling the dough each time. Re-roll and fold twice more without butter. Chill for a final 30 minutes.

5 Roll the dough to a rectangle 45 × 30 cm/18 × 12 inches, trim and halve lengthways. Cut each half into 6 rectangles and brush with beaten egg. Place a chocolate square at one end of each rectangle and roll up to form a sausage. Press the ends together and place, seamside down, on the baking tray (cookie sheet). Cover and leave to rise for 40 minutes in a warm place. Brush with egg and bake in a preheated oven, 220°C/425°F/Gas Mark 7, for 20-25 minutes until golden. Cool on a wire rack. Serve warm or cold.

Choc-Chip Tartlets

These tasty little tartlets will be a big hit with the kids.
Serve as a dessert or a special teatime treat.

Makes 6

INGREDIENTS

50 g/1³/₄ oz toasted hazelnuts
150 g/5¹/₂ oz/1³/₄ cups plain (all-purpose) flour
1 tbsp icing (confectioners') sugar
75 g/2³/₄ oz/¹/₃ cup soft margarine

FILLING:
2 tbsp cornflour (cornstarch)
1 tbsp cocoa powder
1 tbsp caster (superfine) sugar
300 ml/¹/₂ pint/1¹/₄ cups semi-skimmed milk
3 tbsp chocolate and hazelnut spread

25 g/1 oz/2¹/₂ tbsp dark chocolate chips
25 g/1 oz/2¹/₂ tbsp milk chocolate chips
25 g/1 oz/2¹/₂ tbsp white chocolate chips

1 Finely chop the nuts in a food processor. Add the flour, the 1 tbsp sugar and the margarine. Process for a few seconds until the mixture resembles breadcrumbs. Add 2-3 tbsp water and process to form a soft dough. Cover and chill in the freezer for 10 minutes.

2 Roll out the dough and use it to line six 10 cm/4 inch loose-bottomed tartlet tins (pans). Prick the bases with a fork and line them with loosely crumpled foil. Bake in a preheated oven, 200°C/400°F/Gas Mark 6, for 15 minutes. Remove the foil and bake for a further 5 minutes until the pastry cases (pie shells) are crisp and golden. Remove from the oven and leave to cool.

3 Mix together the cornflour (cornstarch), cocoa powder and sugar with enough milk to make a smooth paste. Stir in the remaining milk. Pour into a pan and cook gently over a low heat, stirring until thickened. Stir in the hazelnut and chocolate spread.

4 Mix together the chocolate chips and reserve a quarter. Stir half of the remaining chips into the custard. Cover with damp greaseproof paper and leave until almost cold, then stir in the second half of the chocolate chips. Spoon the mixture into the pastry cases (pie shells) and leave to cool. Decorate with the reserved chips, scattering them over the top.

Chocolate Eclairs

Patisserie cream is the traditional filling for éclairs, but if time is short you can fill them with whipped cream.

Makes about 10

INGREDIENTS

CHOUX PASTRY (PIE DOUGH):
150 ml/^{1}/4 pint/^{2}/3 cup water
60 g/2 oz/^{1}/4 cup butter, cut into small pieces
90 g/3 oz/^{3}/4 cup strong plain (all-purpose) flour, sieved (strained)
2 eggs

PATISSERIE CREAM:
2 eggs, lightly beaten
50 g/1^3/4 oz/4 tbsp caster (superfine) sugar
2 tbsp cornflour (cornstarch)
300 ml/^{1}/2 pint/1^1/4 cups milk
^{1}/4 tsp vanilla flavouring (extract)

ICING:
25 g/1 oz/2 tbsp butter
1 tbsp milk
1 tbsp cocoa powder
100 g/3^1/2 oz/^{1}/2 cup icing (confectioners') sugar
a little white chocolate, melted

1 Lightly grease a baking tray (cookie sheet). Place the water in a saucepan, add the butter and heat gently until the butter melts. Bring to a rolling boil, then remove the pan from the heat and add the flour in one go, beating well until the mixture leaves the sides of the pan and forms a ball. Leave to cool slightly, then gradually beat in the eggs to form a smooth, glossy mixture. Spoon into a large piping bag fitted with a 1 cm/'/2 inch plain nozzle (tip).

2 Sprinkle the tray (sheet) with a little water. Pipe éclairs 7.5 cm/ 3 inches long, spaced well apart. Bake in a preheated oven, 200°C/ 400°F/Gas Mark 6, for 30-35 minutes or until crisp and golden. Make a small slit in each one to let the steam escape; cool on a rack.

3 To make the patisserie cream, whisk the eggs and sugar until thick and creamy, then fold in the cornflour (cornstarch). Heat the milk until almost boiling and pour on to the eggs, whisking. Transfer to the pan and cook over a low heat, stirring until thick. Remove the pan from the heat and stir in the flavouring (extract). Cover with baking parchment and cool. To make the icing, melt the butter with the milk in a pan, remove from the heat and stir in the cocoa and sugar. Split the éclairs lengthways and pipe in the patisserie cream. Spread the icing over the top of the éclair. Spoon over the white chocolate, swirl in and leave to set.

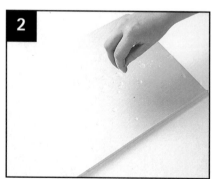

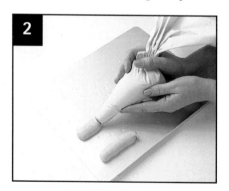

Chocolate Meringues

These melt-in-the-mouth meringues serve for a dessert or a teatime treat. For buffets, make mini meringues, and pile them high in a pyramid for bite-size pure magic.

Makes 8

INGREDIENTS

4 egg whites
225 g/8 oz/1 cup caster (superfine)
   sugar
1 tsp cornflour (cornstarch)
40 g/1¹/₂ oz dark chocolate, grated

TO COMPLETE:
100 g/3¹/₂ oz dark chocolate
150 ml/¹/₄ pint/²/₃ cup double
   (heavy) cream
1 tbsp icing (confectioners') sugar

1 tbsp brandy (optional)

1 Line 2 baking trays (cookie sheets) with baking parchment. Whisk the egg whites until standing in soft peaks, then gradually whisk in half of the sugar. Continue whisking until the mixture is very stiff and glossy.

2 Carefully fold in the remaining sugar, cornflour (cornstarch) and grated chocolate with a metal spoon or spatula.

3 Spoon the mixture into a piping bag fitted with a large star or plain nozzle (tip). Pipe 16 large rosettes or mounds on the lined baking trays (cookie sheets).

4 Bake in a preheated oven, 140°C/275°F/Gas Mark 1, for about 1 hour, changing the position of the baking trays (cookie sheets) halfway through cooking. Without opening the oven door, turn off the oven and leave the meringues to cool in the oven. Once cold, carefully peel away the baking parchment.

5 Melt the dark chocolate and spread it over the base of the meringues. Stand them upside down on a wire rack until the chocolate has set. Whip the cream, icing (confectioners') sugar and brandy (if using), until the cream holds its shape. Spoon into a piping bag and use to sandwich the meringues together in pairs. Serve.

VARIATION

To make mini meringues, use a star shaped nozzle (tip) and pipe about 24 small rosettes. Bake for about 40 minutes until crisp.

Chocolate & Hazelnut Palmiers

These delicious chocolate and hazelnut biscuits (cookies) are very simple to make, yet so effective. For very young children, leave out the chopped nuts.

Makes about 26

INGREDIENTS

375 g/13 oz ready-made puff pastry (pie dough)

8 tbsp chocolate hazelnut spread

50 g/1³/4 oz/¹/2 cup chopped toasted hazelnuts

25 g/1 oz/5 tsp caster (superfine) sugar

1 Lightly grease a baking tray (cookie sheet). On a lightly floured surface, roll out the puff pastry (pie dough) to a rectangle about 37.5 × 23 cm/15 × 9 inches in size.

2 Spread the chocolate hazelnut spread over the pastry (pie dough) using a palette knife, then scatter the chopped hazelnuts over the top.

3 Roll up one long side of the pastry (pie dough) to the centre, then roll up the other side so that they meet in the centre. Where the pieces meet, dampen the edges with a little water to join them. Using a sharp knife, cut into thin slices. Place each slice on to the prepared baking tray (cookie sheet) and flatten slightly with a palette knife. Sprinkle the slices with the caster (superfine) sugar.

4 Bake in a preheated oven, 220°C/425°F/Gas Mark 7, for about 10-15 minutes until golden. Transfer to a wire rack to cool.

COOK'S TIP

Palmiers can be served cold, but they are also delicious served warm.

COOK'S TIP

The biscuits (cookies) can be frozen for up to 3 months in a rigid container.

VARIATION

For an extra chocolate flavour, dip the palmiers in melted dark chocolate to half-cover each biscuit.

Chocolate & Coconut Squares

These biscuits (cookies) consist of a chewy coconut layer resting on a crisp chocolate biscuit base. Cut into squares to serve.

Makes 9

INGREDIENTS

225 g/8 oz dark chocolate digestive biscuits (graham crackers)

75 g/2 ^{3}/4 oz/^{1}/3 cup butter or margarine

170 g/6 oz can evaporated milk

1 egg, beaten

1 tsp vanilla flavouring (extract)

25 g/1 oz/5 tsp caster (superfine) sugar

50 g/1^3/4 oz/^{1}/3 cup self-raising flour, sieved (strained)

125 g/4^1/2 oz/1^1/3 cups desiccated (shredded) coconut

50 g/1^3/4 oz dark chocolate (optional)

---

1 Grease a shallow 20 cm/ 8 inch square cake tin (pan) and line the base.

2 Crush the biscuits (crackers) in a polythene bag with a rolling pin or process them in a food processor.

3 Melt the butter or margarine in a saucepan and stir in the crushed biscuits (crackers) until well combined.

4 Press the mixture into the base of the cake tin (pan).

5 Beat together the evaporated milk, egg, vanilla and sugar until smooth. Stir in the flour and desiccated (shredded) coconut. Pour over the biscuit base and level the top.

6 Bake in a preheated oven, 190°C/375°F/Gas Mark 5, for 30 minutes or until the coconut topping is firm and just golden.

7 Leave to cool in the cake tin (pan) for about 5 minutes, then cut into squares. Leave to cool completely in the tin (pan).

8 Carefully remove the squares from the tin (pan) and place them on a board. Melt the dark chocolate (if using) and drizzle it over the squares to decorate them. Leave the chocolate to set before serving.

COOK'S TIP

Store the squares in an airtight tin for up to 4 days. They can be frozen, undecorated, for up to 2 months. Defrost at room temperature.

Chocolate & Coconut Cookies

Chocolate and coconut combine well in these delicious melt-in-the-mouth biscuits (cookies). They are finished off with a simple gooey icing and a generous sprinkling of coconut.

Makes about 24

INGREDIENTS

125 g/4^1/$_2$ oz/^{1}/$_3$ cup soft margarine
1 tsp vanilla flavouring (extract)
90 g/3 oz/6 tbsp icing
   (confectioners') sugar, sieved
   (strained)

125 g/4^1/$_2$ oz/1 cup plain (all-
   purpose) flour
2 tbsp cocoa powder
50 g/1^3/$_4$ oz/^{2}/$_3$ cup desiccated
   (shredded) coconut

25 g/1 oz/2 tbsp butter
100 g/3^1/$_2$ oz white marshmallows
25 g/1 oz/^{1}/$_3$ cup desiccated
   (shredded) coconut
a little dark chocolate, melted

1 Lightly grease a baking tray (cookie sheet). Beat together the margarine, vanilla flavouring (extract) and icing (confectioners') sugar in a mixing bowl until light and fluffy. Sift together the flour and cocoa powder and beat it into the mixture with the coconut.

2 Roll rounded teaspoons of the mixture into balls and place on the prepared baking tray (cookie sheet), allowing room for the biscuits (cookies) to spread during cooking.

3 Flatten the rounds slightly and bake in a preheated oven, 180°C/350°F/Gas Mark 4, for 12-15 minutes until just firm.

4 Leave to cool on the baking tray (cookie sheet) for a few minutes before transferring to a wire rack to cool completely.

5 Combine the butter and marshmallows in a small saucepan and heat gently, stirring until melted and well combined. Spread a little of the icing mixture over each biscuit and dip in the coconut. Leave to set. Decorate the biscuits (cookies) with a little melted chocolate and leave to set before serving.

COOK'S TIP

Store these biscuits (cookies) in an airtight container for about 1 week. Alternatively, they can be frozen, undecorated, for up to 2 months.

Chocolate Crispy Bites

A favourite with children, this version of crispy bites have been given a new twist which is sure to be popular.

Makes 16

INGREDIENTS

WHITE LAYER:
50 g/1³/4 oz/4 tbsp butter
1 tbsp golden (light corn) syrup
150 g/5¹/2 oz white chocolate

50 g/1³/4 oz toasted rice cereal

DARK LAYER:
50 g/1³/4 oz/4 tbsp butter
2 tbsp golden (light corn) syrup

125 g/dark chocolate, broken into
  small pieces
75 g/2³/4 oz toasted rice cereal

1 Grease a 20 cm/8 inch square cake tin (pan) and line with baking parchment.

2 To make the white chocolate layer, melt the butter, golden (light corn) syrup and chocolate in a bowl set over a saucepan of gently simmering water.

3 Remove from the heat and stir in the rice cereal until it is well combined .

4 Press into the prepared tin (pan) and level the surface.

5 To make the dark chocolate layer, melt the butter, golden (light corn) syrup and dark chocolate in a bowl set over a pan of gently simmering water.

6 Remove from the heat and stir in the rice cereal until it is well coated. Pour the dark chocolate layer over the hardened white chocolate layer and chill until the top layer has hardened.

7 Turn out of the cake tin (pan) and cut into small squares, using a sharp knife.

COOK'S TIP

These bites can be made up to 4 days ahead. Keep them covered in the refrigerator until ready to use.

Dutch Macaroons

These unusual biscuit (cookie) treats are delicious served with coffee. They also make an ideal dessert biscuit (cookie) to serve with ice cream.

Makes about 20

INGREDIENTS

rice paper
2 egg whites

225 g/8 oz/1 cup caster (superfine) sugar

175 g/6 oz/1²/₃ cups ground almonds
225 g/8 oz dark chocolate

1 Cover 2 baking trays (cookie sheets) with rice paper. Whisk the egg whites in a large mixing bowl until stiff, then fold in the sugar and ground almonds.

2 Place the mixture in a large piping bag fitted with a 1 cm/ ¹/₂ inch plain nozzle (tip) and pipe fingers, about 7.5 cm/3 inches long, allowing space for the mixture to spread during cooking.

3 Bake in a preheated oven, 180°C/350°F/Gas Mark 4, for 15-20 minutes until golden. Transfer to a wire rack and leave to cool. Remove the excess rice paper from around the edges.

4 Melt the chocolate and dip the base of each biscuit into the chocolate. Place the macaroons on a sheet of baking parchment and leave to set.

5 Drizzle any remaining chocolate over the top of the biscuits (cookies). Leave to set before serving.

COOK'S TIP

Rice paper is edible so you can break off the excess from around the edge of the biscuits (cookies). Remove it completely before dipping in the chocolate, if you prefer.

VARIATION

Almonds are most commonly used in macaroons, but they can be made with other ground nuts, such as hazelnuts.

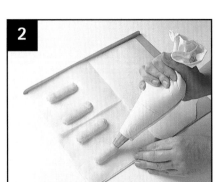

Chocolate Orange Biscuits (Cookies)

These are delicious melt-in-the-mouth chocolate cookies with a tangy orange icing. Children love these cookies, especially if different shaped cutters are used.

Makes about 30

INGREDIENTS

75 g/2 ³/₄ oz/¹/₃ cup butter, softened
75 g/2 ³/₄ oz/¹/₃ cup caster
   (superfine) sugar
1 egg
1 tbsp milk

225 g/8 oz/2 cups plain (all-purpose)
   flour
25 g/1 oz/¹/₄ cup cocoa powder

ICING:
175 g/6 oz/1 cup icing
   (confectioners') sugar, sifted
3 tbsp orange juice
a little dark chocolate, melted

1 Line 2 baking trays (cookie sheets) with sheets of baking parchment.

2 Beat together the butter and sugar until light and fluffy. Beat in the egg and milk until well combined. Sift together the flour and cocoa powder and gradually mix together to form a soft dough. Use your fingers to incorporate the last of the flour and bring the dough together.

3 Roll out the dough on to a lightly floured surface until 6 mm/¹/₄ inch thick. Using a 5 cm/ 2 inch fluted round cutter, cut out as many cookies as you can. Re-roll the dough trimmings and cut out more cookies.

4 Place the cookies on the prepared baking tray (cookie sheet) and bake in a preheated oven, 180°C/350°F/Gas Mark 4, for 10-12 minutes or until golden.

5 Leave the cookies to cool on the baking tray (cookie sheet) for a few minutes, then transfer to a wire rack to cool completely.

6 To make the icing, place the icing (confectioners') sugar in a bowl and stir in enough orange juice to form a thin icing that will coat the back of a spoon. Spread the icing over the cookies and leave to set. Drizzle with melted chocolate. Leave the chocolate to set before serving.

Chocolate Caramel Squares

Wonderfully rich, it is difficult to say 'No' to these biscuits (cookies), which consist of a crunchy base, a creamy caramel filling and a chocolate top.

Makes 16

INGREDIENTS

100 g/3^1/$_2$ oz/generous ^{1}/$_3$ cup soft margarine
50 g/1^3/$_4$ oz/4 tbsp light muscovado sugar
125 g/4^1/$_2$ oz/1 cup plain (all-purpose) flour

40 g/1^1/$_2$ oz/^{1}/$_2$ cup rolled oats

CARAMEL FILLING:
25 g/1 oz/2 tbsp butter
25 g/1 oz/2 tbsp light muscovado sugar

200 g/7 oz can condensed milk

TOPPING:
100 g/3^1/$_2$ oz dark chocolate
25 g/1 oz white chocolate (optional)

1 Beat together the margarine and muscovado sugar in a bowl until light and fluffy. Beat in the flour and the rolled oats. Use your fingertips to bring the mixture together, if necessary.

2 Press the mixture into the base of a shallow 20 cm/ 8 inch square cake tin (pan).

3 Bake in a preheated oven, 180°C/350°F/Gas Mark 4, for 25 minutes or until just golden and firm. Cool in the tin (pan).

4 Place the ingredients for the caramel filling in a pan and heat gently, stirring until the sugar has dissolved and the ingredients combine. Bring slowly to the boil over a very low heat, then boil very gently for 3-4 minutes, stirring constantly until thickened.

5 Pour the caramel filling over the biscuit base in the tin (pan) and leave to set.

6 Melt the dark chocolate and spread it over the caramel. If

using the white chocolate, melt it and pipe lines of white chocolate over the dark chocolate. Using a cocktail stick (toothpick) or a skewer, feather the white chocolate into the dark chocolate. Leave to set. Cut into squares to serve.

COOK'S TIP

If liked, you can line the tin (pan) (pan) with baking parchment so that the biscuit can be lifted out before cutting into pieces.

Chocolate Chip Flapjacks

Turn ordinary flapjacks into something special with the addition of some chocolate chips. Dark chocolate chips are used here, but you could use milk chocolate or white chocolate chips, if preferred.

Makes 12

INGREDIENTS

125 g/4¹/₂ oz/¹/₂ cup butter
75 g/2³/₄ oz/¹/₃ cup caster
 (superfine) sugar
1 tbsp golden (light corn) syrup

350 g/12 oz/4 cups rolled oats
75 g/2³/₄ oz/¹/₂ cup dark chocolate
 chips

50 g/1³/₄ oz/¹/₃ cup sultanas (golden
 raisins)

1 Lightly grease a shallow 20 cm/8 inch square cake tin (pan).

2 Place the butter, caster (superfine) sugar and golden (light corn) syrup in a saucepan and cook over a low heat, stirring until the butter and sugar melt and the mixture is well combined.

3 Remove the pan from the heat and stir in the rolled oats until they are well coated. Add the chocolate chips and the sultanas (golden raisins) and mix well to combine everything.

4 Turn into the prepared tin (pan) and press down well.

5 Bake in a preheated oven, 180°C/350°F/Gas Mark 4, for 30 minutes. Cool slightly, then mark into fingers. When almost cold cut into bars or squares and transfer to a wire rack until cold.

COOK'S TIP

The flapjacks will keep in an airtight container for up to 1 week, but they are so delicious they are unlikely to last that long!

VARIATION

For a really special flapjack, replace some of the oats with chopped nuts or sunflower seeds and a little extra dried fruit.

Chocolate Chip Cookies

No chocolate cook's repertoire would be complete without a chocolate chip cookie recipe.
This is sure to be a favourite as the basic recipe can be used to make several variations.

Makes about 18

INGREDIENTS

175 g/6 oz/1¹/₂ cups plain (all-purpose) flour

1 tsp baking powder

125 g/4¹/₂ oz/¹/₂ cup soft margarine

90 g/3 oz/generous ¹/₂ cup light muscovado sugar

60 g/2 oz/¹/₄ cup caster (superfine) sugar

¹/₂ tsp vanilla flavouring (extract)

1 egg

125 g/4¹/₂ oz/²/₃ cup dark chocolate chips

1 Lightly grease 2 baking trays (cookie sheets).

2 Place all of the ingredients in a large mixing bowl and beat until well combined.

3 Place tablespoonfuls of the mixture on to the baking trays (cookie sheets), spacing them well apart to allow for spreading during cooking.

4 Bake in a preheated oven, 190°C/375°F/Gas Mark 5, for 10-12 minutes or until the cookies are golden brown.

5 Using a palette knife (spatula), transfer the cookies to a wire rack to cool completely.

VARIATIONS

For Choc & Nut Cookies, add 40 g/1¹/₂ oz/¹/₂ cup chopped hazelnuts to the basic mixture.

For Double Choc Cookies, beat in 40 g/1¹/₂ oz melted dark chocolate.

For White Chocolate Chip Cookies, use white chocolate chips instead of the dark chocolate chips.

VARIATIONS

For Mixed Chocolate Chip Cookies, use a mixture of dark, milk and white chocolate chips in the basic mixture.

For Chocolate Chip & Coconut Cookies, add 25 g/1 oz/¹/₃ cup desiccated (shredded) coconut to the basic mixture.

For Chocolate Chip & Raisin Cookies, add 40 g/1¹/₂ oz/ 5 tbsp raisins to the basic mixture.

Chocolate Shortbread

*This buttery chocolate shortbread is the perfect addition
to the biscuit tin of any chocoholic.*

Makes 12

INGREDIENTS

175 g/6 oz/1¹/₂ cups plain (all-
  purpose) flour
1 tbsp cocoa powder

50 g/1³/₄ oz/4 tbsp caster (superfine)
  sugar
150 g/5¹/₂oz/²/₃ cup butter, softened

50 g/1³/₄ oz dark chocolate, chopped
  finely

1 Lightly grease a baking tray (cookie sheet).

2 Place all of the ingredients in a large mixing bowl and beat together until they form a dough. Knead the dough lightly.

3 Place the dough on the prepared baking tray (cookie sheet) and roll or press out to form a 20 cm/8 inch circle.

4 Pinch the edges of the dough with your fingertips to form a decorative edge. Prick the dough all over with a fork and mark into 12 wedges, using a sharp knife.

5 Bake in a preheated oven, 160°C/325°F/Gas Mark 3, for 40 minutes until firm and golden. Leave to cool slightly before cutting into wedges. Transfer to a wire rack to cool completely.

VARIATION

For round shortbread cookies, roll out the dough on a lightly floured surface to 8 mm/¹/₃ inch thick. Cut out 7.5 cm/3 inch rounds with a biscuit (cookie) cutter. Transfer to a greased baking tray (cookie sheet) and bake as above. If liked, coat half the biscuit in melted chocolate.

VARIATION

The shortbread dough can be pressed into a floured shortbread mould (mold) and turned out on to the baking tray (cookie sheet) before baking.

Malted Chocolate Wedges

These are perfect with a bedtime drink, although you can enjoy these
tasty biscuit (cookie) wedges at any time of the day.

Makes 16

INGREDIENTS

100 g/3¹/₂ oz/generous ¹/₃ cup butter
2 tbsp golden (light corn) syrup
2 tbsp malted chocolate drink

225 g/8 oz malted milk biscuits
(cookies)
75 g/2³/₄ oz milk or dark chocolate,
broken into pieces

25 g/1 oz/2 tbsp icing
(confectioners') sugar
2 tbsp milk

1 Grease a shallow 18 cm/
7 inch round cake tin (pan)
or flan tin (pan) and line the base.

2 Place the butter, golden (light
corn) syrup and malted
chocolate drink in a small pan and
heat gently, stirring all the time
until the butter has melted and the
mixture is well combined.

3 Crush the biscuits (cookies)
in a plastic bag with a rolling
pin, or process them in a food
processor until they form crumbs.
Stir the crumbs into the chocolate
mixture and mix well.

4 Press the mixture into the
prepared tin (pan) and chill in
the refrigerator until firm.

5 Place the chocolate pieces in a
small heatproof bowl with the
icing (confectioners') sugar and
the milk. Place the bowl over a pan
of gently simmering water and stir
until the chocolate melts and the
mixture is combined.

6 Spread the chocolate icing
over the biscuit (cookie) base
and leave to set in the tin (pan).
Using a sharp knife, cut into
wedges to serve.

VARIATION

Add chopped pecan nuts
to the biscuit (cookie) crumb
mixture in step 3, if liked.

Chocolate Chequer-board Cookies

Children will love these two-tone chocolate biscuits (cookies). If you do not mind a little mess, let them help to form the biscuits (cookies).

Makes about 18

INGREDIENTS

175 g/6 oz/³/₄ cup butter, softened
75 g/2³/₄ oz/6 tbsp icing (confectioners') sugar

1 teaspoon vanilla flavouring (extract) or grated rind of ¹/₂ orange

250 g/9 oz/2¹/₄ cups plain (all-purpose) flour
25 g/1 oz dark chocolate, melted
a little beaten egg white

1 Lightly grease a baking tray (cookie sheet). Beat the butter and icing (confectioners') sugar in a mixing bowl until light and fluffy. Beat in the vanilla flavouring (extract) or the grated orange rind.

2 Gradually beat in the flour to form a soft dough. Use your fingers to incorporate the last of the flour and bring the dough together.

3 Divide the dough into 2 equal pieces and beat the melted chocolate into one half.

Keeping each half of the dough separate, cover and leave to chill for about 30 minutes.

4 Roll out each piece of dough to a rectangle about 7.5 × 20 cm/ 3 × 8 inches long and 3 cm/1¹/₂ inches thick. Brush one piece of dough with a little egg white and place the other on top.

5 Cut the block of dough in half lengthways and turn over one half. Brush the side of one strip with egg white and butt the other up to it, so that it resembles a chequer-board.

6 Cut the block into thin slices and place each slice flat on the baking tray (cookie sheet), allowing enough room for them to spread a little during cooking.

7 Bake in a preheated oven, 180°C/350°F/Gas Mark 4, for about 10 minutes until just firm. Leave to cool on the baking trays (cookie sheets) for a few minutes, before carefully transferring to a wire rack with a palette knife (spatula). Leave to cool completely.

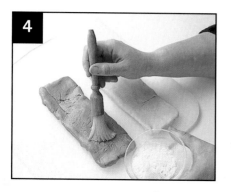

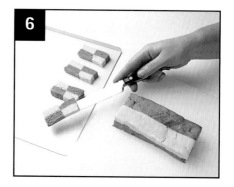

Viennese Chocolate Fingers

These biscuits (cookies) have a fabulously light, melting texture. You can leave them plain, but for real chocolate indulgence dip in chocolate to decorate.

Makes about 18

INGREDIENTS

125 g/4^1/$_2$ oz/^{1}/$_2$ cup unsalted butter

75 g/2^3/$_4$ oz/6 tbsp icing (confectioners') sugar

175 g/6 oz/1^1/$_2$ cups self-raising flour, sieved (strained)

25 g/1 oz/3 tbsp cornflour (cornstarch)

200 g/7 oz dark chocolate

1 Lightly grease 2 baking trays (cookie sheets). Beat the butter and sugar in a mixing bowl until light and fluffy. Gradually beat in the flour and cornflour (cornstarch).

2 Melt 75 g/2^3/$_4$ oz of the dark chocolate and beat into the biscuit dough.

3 Place in a piping bag fitted with a large star nozzle (tip) and pipe fingers about 5 cm/ 2 inches long on the baking trays (cookie sheets), slightly spaced apart to allow for spreading.

4 Bake in a preheated oven, 190°C/375°F/Gas Mark 5, for 12-15 minutes. Leave to cool slightly on the baking trays (cookie sheets), then transfer with a palette knife (spatula) to a wire rack and leave to cool completely.

5 Melt the remaining chocolate and dip one end of each biscuit (cookie) in the chocolate, allowing the excess to drip back into the bowl.

6 Place the biscuits (cookies) on a sheet of baking parchment and leave to set before serving.

COOK'S TIP

If the biscuit (cookie) dough is too thick to pipe, beat in a little milk to thin it out a little.

VARIATION

Dip the base of each biscuit in melted chocolate and leave to set. Sandwich the biscuits (cookies) together in pairs with a little butter cream.

Chocolate Pretzels

If you thought of pretzels as savouries, then think again. These are fun to make
and prove that pretzels come in a sweet variety, too.

Makes about 30

INGREDIENTS

100 g/3¹/₂ oz/generous ¹/₃ cup
  unsalted butter
100 g/3¹/₂ oz/7 tbsp caster
  (superfine) sugar
1 egg

225 g/8 oz/2 cups plain (all-purpose)
  flour
25 g/1 oz/¹/₄ cup cocoa powder

TO FINISH:
15 g/¹/₂ oz/1 tbsp butter
100 g/3¹/₂ oz dark chocolate
icing (confectioners') sugar, to dust

1 Lightly grease a baking tray (cookie sheet). Beat together the butter and sugar in a mixing bowl until light and fluffy. Beat in the egg.

2 Sift together the flour and cocoa powder and gradually beat in to form a soft dough. Use your fingers to incorporate the last of the flour and bring the dough together. Chill for 15 minutes.

3 Break pieces from the dough and roll into thin sausage shapes about 10 cm/4 inches long and 6 mm/¹/₄ inch thick. Twist into pretzel shapes by making a circle, then twist the ends through each other to form a letter 'B'.

4 Place on the prepared baking tray (cookie sheet), slightly spaced apart to allow for spreading during cooking.

5 Bake in a preheated oven, 190°C/375°F/Gas Mark 5, for 8-12 minutes. Leave the pretzels to cool slightly on the baking tray (cookie sheet), then transfer to a wire rack to cool completely.

6 Melt the butter and chocolate in a bowl set over a pan of gently simmering water, stirring to combine.

7 Dip half of each pretzel into the chocolate and allow the excess chocolate to drip back into the bowl. Place the pretzels on a sheet of baking parchment and leave to set.

8 When set, dust the non-chocolate coated side of each pretzel with icing (confectioners') sugar before serving.

Chocolate Wheatmeals

A good everyday biscuit, these will keep well in an airtight container for at least 1 week. Dip in white, milk or dark chocolate.

Makes about 20

INGREDIENTS

75 g/2 $^3/_4$ oz/$^1/_3$ cup butter
100 g/3$^1/_2$ oz/7 tbsp demerara
  (brown crystal) sugar
1 egg

25 g/1 oz wheatgerm
125 g/4$^1/_2$ oz/1 cup wholemeal
  (whole wheat) self-raising flour

60 g/2 oz/$^1/_2$ cup self raising flour,
  sieved (strained)
125 g/4$^1/_2$ oz chocolate

1 Lightly grease a baking tray (cookie sheet). Beat the butter and sugar until fluffy. Add the egg and beat well. Stir in the wheatgerm and flours. Bring the mixture together with your hands.

2 Roll rounded teaspoons of the mixture into balls and place on the prepared baking tray (cookie sheet), allowing room for the biscuits (cookies) to spread during cooking.

3 Flatten the biscuits (cookies) slightly with the prongs of a fork. Bake in a preheated oven, 180°C/350°F/Gas Mark 4, for 15-20 minutes until golden. Leave to cool on the tray (sheet) for a few minutes before transferring to a wire rack to cool completely.

4 Melt the chocolate, then dip each biscuit (cookie) in the chocolate to cover the bases and come a little way up the sides. Leave the excess to drip back into the bowl.

5 Place the biscuits (cookies) on a sheet of baking parchment and leave to set in a cool place before serving.

COOK'S TIP

These biscuits (cookies) can be frozen very successfully. Freeze them at the end of step 3 for up to 3 months. Defrost and then dip them in melted chocolate.

Hot Puddings

Chocolate is comforting at anytime but no more so than when served in a steaming hot pudding. It is hard to think of anything more warming, comforting and homely than tucking into a steamed hot Chocolate Fudge Pudding or a Hot Chocolate Soufflé. The child in us will love the chocolate addition to nursery favourites such as Chocolate Bread & Butter Pudding. In fact, there are several old favourites that have been given the chocolate treatment, bringing them bang up to date and putting them on the chocolate lovers map.

When you are feeling in need of something a little more sophisticated, try the new-style Chocolate Apple Pancake Stack, or Chocolate Pear & Almond Flan, which might be more in keeping. Or try Chocolate Zabaglione for a sophisticated creamy, warm dessert set to get your taste buds in a whirl!

This chapter is packed full of chocolate delights, with different tastes and textures to add warmth to any day.

Chocolate Queen of Puddings

An old time favourite with an up-to-date twist, this pudding makes the perfect end to a special family meal.

Serves 4

INGREDIENTS

50 g/1³/₄ oz dark chocolate
450 ml/16 fl oz/2 cups chocolate-
  flavoured milk

100 g/3¹/₂ oz/1³/₄ cups fresh white
  or wholemeal (whole wheat)
  breadcrumbs

125 g/4¹/₂ oz/¹/₂ cup caster
  (superfine) sugar
2 eggs, separated
4 tbsp black cherry jam

1 Break the chocolate into small pieces and place in a saucepan with the chocolate-flavoured milk. Heat gently, stirring until the chocolate melts. Bring almost to the boil, then remove the pan from the heat.

2 Place the breadcrumbs in a large mixing bowl with 25 g/ 1 oz/5 tsp of the sugar. Pour over the chocolate milk and mix well. Beat in the egg yolks.

3 Spoon into a 1.1 litre/2 pint/ 5 cup pie dish and bake in a preheated oven, 180°C/350°F/

Gas Mark 4, for 25-30 minutes or until set and firm to the touch.

4 Whisk the egg whites in a large grease-free bowl until standing in soft peaks. Gradually whisk in the remaining caster (superfine) sugar and whisk until you have a glossy, thick meringue.

5 Spread the black cherry jam over the surface of the chocolate mixture and pile or pipe the meringue on top. Return the pudding to the oven for about 15 minutes or until the meringue is crisp and golden.

VARIATION

If you prefer, add 40 g/1¹/₂ oz/¹/₂ cup desiccated (shredded) coconut to the breadcrumbs and omit the jam.

Chocolate Eve's Pudding with Bitter Chocolate Sauce

Eve's Pudding is traditionally made with apples, but here it is made with raspberries as well and topped with a moist white chocolate sponge. Served with a bitter chocolate sauce, the taste is superb.

Serves 4

INGREDIENTS

225 g/8 oz fresh or frozen raspberries
2 eating apples, peeled, cored and
  sliced thickly
4 tbsp seedless raspberry jam
2 tbsp port (optional)

SPONGE TOPPING:
50 g/1^3/4 oz/4 tbsp soft margarine
50 g/1^3/4 oz/4 tbsp caster (superfine)
  sugar
75 g/2^3/4 oz/^{2}/3 cup self-raising
  flour, sieved (strained)
50 g/1^3/4 oz white chocolate, grated

1 egg
2 tbsp milk

BITTER CHOCOLATE SAUCE:
90 g/3 oz dark chocolate
150 ml/^{1}/4 pint/^{2}/3 cup single (light)
  cream

1 Place the apple slices and raspberries in a shallow 1.1 litre/2 pint/5 cup ovenproof dish.

2 Place the raspberry jam and port (if using) in a small pan and heat gently until the jam melts and combines with the port. Pour the mixture over the fruit.

3 Place all of the ingredients for the sponge topping in a large mixing bowl and beat until the mixture is smooth.

4 Spoon the sponge mixture over the fruit and level the top. Bake in a preheated oven, 180°C/350°F/Gas Mark 4, for 40-45 minutes or until the sponge is springy to the touch.

5 To make the sauce, break the chocolate into small pieces and place in a heavy-based saucepan with the cream. Heat gently, beating until a smooth sauce is formed. Serve warm with the pudding.

VARIATION

Use dark chocolate in the sponge and top with apricot halves, covered with peach schnapps and apricot conserve.

Mini Chocolate Ginger Puddings with Chocolate Custard

Individual puddings always look more professional and are quicker to cook.
If you do not have mini pudding basins, use small teacups instead.

Serves 4

INGREDIENTS

100 g/3 ^{1}/$_2$ oz/generous ^{1}/$_3$ cup soft
   margarine
100 g/3 ^{1}/$_2$ oz/^{3}/$_4$ cup self-raising
   flour, sieved (strained)
100 g/3 ^{1}/$_2$ oz/7 tbsp caster
   (superfine) sugar
2 eggs

25 g/1 oz/^{1}/$_4$ cup cocoa powder,
   sieved (strained)
25 g/1 oz dark chocolate
50 g/1^3/$_4$ oz stem ginger

CHOCOLATE CUSTARD:
2 egg yolks

1 tbsp caster (superfine) sugar
1 tbsp cornflour (cornstarch)
300 ml/^{1}/$_2$ pint/1^1/$_4$ cups milk
100 g/3^1/$_2$ oz dark chocolate, broken
   into pieces
icing (confectioners') sugar, to dust

1 Lightly grease 4 individual pudding basins. Place the margarine, flour, sugar, eggs and cocoa powder in a mixing bowl and beat until well combined and smooth. Chop the chocolate and ginger and stir into the mixture.

2 Spoon the cake mixture into the prepared basins and level the top. The mixture should three-quarters fill the basins.

Cover the basins with discs of baking parchment and cover with a pleated sheet of foil. Steam for 45 minutes until the puddings are cooked and springy to the touch.

3 Meanwhile, make the custard. Beat together the egg yolks, sugar and cornflour (cornstarch) to form a smooth paste. Heat the milk until boiling and pour over the egg mixture. Return to the pan

and cook over a very low heat stirring until thick. Remove from the heat and beat in the chocolate. Stir until the chocolate melts.

4 Lift the puddings from the steamer, run a knife around the edge of the basins and turn out on to serving plates. Dust with sugar and drizzle some chocolate custard over the top. Serve the remaining custard separately.

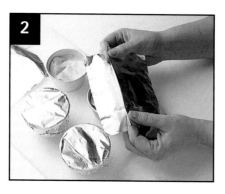

Chocolate Bread & Butter Pudding

This all-time favourite nursery pudding is given a new twist, bringing it right up to date. Brioche gives the pudding a lovely rich flavour, but this recipe also works well with soft-baked batch bread.

Serves 4

INGREDIENTS

225 g/8 oz brioche
15 g/$^{1}/_2$ oz/1 tbsp butter
50 g/1$^{3}/_4$ oz dark chocolate chips

1 egg
2 egg yolks

50 g/1$^{3}/_4$ oz/4 tbsp caster (superfine) sugar
410 g/15 oz can light evaporated milk

1 Cut the brioche into thin slices. Lightly butter one side of each slice.

2 Place a layer of brioche, buttered-side down, in the bottom of a shallow ovenproof dish. Sprinkle a few chocolate chips over the top.

3 Continue layering the brioche and chocolate chips, finishing with a layer of bread on top.

4 Whisk together the egg, egg yolks and sugar until well combined. Heat the milk in a small saucepan until it just begins to simmer. Gradually add to the egg mixture, whisking well.

5 Pour the custard over the pudding and leave to stand for 5 minutes. Press the brioche down into the milk.

6 Place in a roasting tin (pan) and fill with boiling water to come halfway up the side of the dish (this is known as a *bain-marie*).

7 Bake in a preheated oven, 180°C/350°F/Gas Mark 4, for 30 minutes or until the custard has set. Leave to cool for 5 minutes before serving.

COOK'S TIP

The pudding can be made a few hours ahead and baked when required. It also tastes good cold.

VARIATION

For a double-chocolate pudding, heat the milk with 1 tbsp of cocoa powder, stirring until well dissolved then continue from step 4.

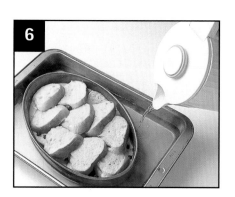

Chocolate French Toasties

*There is something very more-ish about these delicious chocolate toasties,
served with a little whipped cream and raspberry jam sauce.*

Serves 4-6

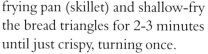
INGREDIENTS

50 g/1³/₄ oz dark chocolate
150 ml/¹/₄ pint/²/₃ cup milk
1 egg
4 tbsp seedless raspberry jam

2 tbsp rum (optional)
8 thick slices white bread
butter or oil, for shallow-frying
¹/₂ tsp ground cinnamon

40 g/1¹/₂ oz/3 tbsp caster (superfine)
   sugar
a little whipped cream, to serve

1 Break the chocolate into small pieces and place in a small pan with the milk. Heat gently, stirring until the chocolate melts. Leave to cool slightly.

2 Beat the egg in a large mixing bowl and whisk in the warm chocolate milk.

3 Heat the raspberry jam gently and stir in the rum, if using. Set aside and keep warm.

4 Remove the crusts from the bread, cut into triangles and dip each one into the chocolate mixture. Heat the butter or oil in a frying pan (skillet) and shallow-fry the bread triangles for 2-3 minutes until just crispy, turning once.

5 Mix together the cinnamon and caster (superfine) sugar and sprinkle it over the toasties. Serve with the hot jam sauce and a little whipped cream.

COOK'S TIP

*Young children adore this dessert.
Cut the bread into fingers to make
it easier for them to handle.*

VARIATION

*If you wish, try this recipe
using brioche or fruit bread for
a tasty variation.*

Chocolate Fudge Pudding

This fabulous steamed pudding, served with a rich chocolate fudge sauce, is perfect for cold winter days – and it can be made in double quick time in the microwave, if you have one.

Serves 6

INGREDIENTS

150 g/5^1/$_2$ oz/generous ^{1}/$_3$ cup soft
   margarine
150 g/5^1/$_2$ oz/1^1/$_4$ cups self-raising
   flour
150 g/5^1/$_2$ oz/^{1}/$_2$ cup golden (light
   corn) syrup

3 eggs
25 g/1 oz/^{1}/$_4$ cup cocoa powder

CHOCOLATE FUDGE SAUCE:
100 g/3^1/$_2$ oz dark chocolate
125 ml/4 fl oz/^{1}/$_2$ cup sweetened
   condensed milk
4 tbsp double (heavy) cream

1 Lightly grease a 1.2 litre/
2 pint/5 cup pudding basin.

2 Place the ingredients for the sponge in a mixing bowl and beat until well combined and smooth.

3 Spoon into the prepared basin and level the top. Cover with a disc of baking parchment and tie a pleated sheet of foil over the basin. Steam for 1^1/$_2$-2 hours until the pudding is cooked and springy to the touch.

4 To make the sauce, break the chocolate into small pieces and place in a small pan with the condensed milk. Heat gently, stirring until the chocolate melts.

5 Remove the pan from the heat and stir in the double (heavy) cream.

6 To serve the pudding, turn it out on to a serving plate and pour over a little of the chocolate fudge sauce. Serve the remaining sauce separately.

COOK'S TIP

To cook the cake in the microwave, cook it, uncovered, on High for 4 minutes, turning the basin once. Leave to stand for at least 5 minutes before turning out. Whilst the pudding is standing, make the sauce. Break the chocolate into pieces and place in a microwave-proof bowl with the milk. Cook on High for 1 minute, then stir until the chocolate melts. Stir in the double (heavy) cream and serve.

Chocolate Fruit Crumble

A popular dessert, the addition of chocolate in the topping makes it even more of a treat.
A good way of enticing children to eat a fruit dessert.

Serves 4

INGREDIENTS

400 g/14 oz can apricots, in natural juice
450 g/1 lb cooking apples, peeled and sliced thickly

100 g/3^1/$_2$ oz/^{3}/$_4$ cup plain (all-purpose) flour
75 g/2^3/$_4$ oz/^{1}/$_3$ cup butter
50 g/1^3/$_4$ oz/^{2}/$_3$ cup porridge oats

50 g/1^3/$_4$ oz/4 tbsp caster (superfine) sugar
100 g/3^1/$_2$ oz/^{2}/$_3$ cup chocolate chips

1 Lightly grease an ovenproof dish with a little butter or margarine.

2 Drain the apricots, reserving 4 tbsp of the juice. Place the apples and apricots in the prepared ovenproof dish with the reserved apricot juice and toss to mix.

3 Sieve (strain) the flour into a mixing bowl. Cut the butter into small cubes and rub in with your fingertips until the mixture resembles fine breadcrumbs. Stir in the porridge oats, sugar and chocolate chips.

4 Sprinkle the crumble mixture over the apples and apricots and level the top roughly. Do not press the crumble into the fruit.

5 Bake in a preheated oven, 350°F/180°C/Gas Mark 4, for 40-45 minutes or until the topping is golden. Serve hot or cold.

COOK'S TIP

You can use dark, milk or white chocolate chips in this recipe or a mixture of all three.

VARIATION

Other fruits can be used to make this crumble – fresh pears mixed with fresh or frozen raspberries work well. If you do not use canned fruit, add 4 tablespoons of orange juice to the fresh fruit.

VARIATION

For a double chocolate crumble, replace 1-2 tablespoons of flour with cocoa powder.

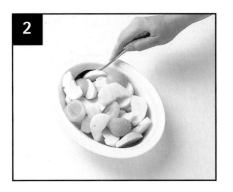

Poached Pears with Mascarpone Chocolate Sauce

This is a very simple, elegant dessert which can be served hot or cold. The pears can be poached up to 2 days in advance and stored in their poaching juices in the refrigerator.

Serves 6

INGREDIENTS

6 firm ripe pears
100 g/3$^{1}/_{2}$ oz/7 tbsp caster
   (superfine) sugar
2 cinnamon sticks

rind of 1 orange
2 cloves
1 bottle rosé wine

CHOCOLATE SAUCE:
175 g/6 oz dark chocolate
250 g/9 oz mascarpone cheese
2 tbsp orange-flavoured liqueur

1 Carefully peel the pears, leaving the stalk intact.

2 Place the sugar, cinnamon, sticks, orange rind, cloves and wine in a saucepan that will hold the 6 pears snugly.

3 Heat gently until the sugar has dissolved, then add the pears to the liquid and bring to a simmer. Cover and poach gently for 20 minutes. If serving them cold, leave the pears to cool in the liquid, then chill until required. If serving hot, leave the pears in the hot liquid whilst preparing the chocolate sauce.

4 To make the sauce, melt the chocolate. Beat together the cheese and the orange-flavoured liqueur. Beat the cheese mixture into the chocolate.

5 Remove the pears from the poaching liquid and place on a serving plate. Add a generous spoonful of sauce on the side and serve the remainder separately.

COOK'S TIP

There is no need to waste the tasty poaching liquid. Boil it rapidly in a clean pan for about 10 minutes to reduce to a syrup. Use the syrup to sweeten a fresh fruit salad or spoon it over ice cream.

COOK'S TIP

Rosettes of cream can be piped on to the dessert, if liked.

Saucy Chocolate Pudding

In this recipe, the mixture separates out during cooking to produce a cream sponge topping and a delicious chocolate sauce on the bottom.

Serves 4

INGREDIENTS

300 ml/^{1}/$_2$ pint/1^1/$_4$ cups milk
75 g/2^3/$_4$ oz dark chocolate
^{1}/$_2$ tsp vanilla flavouring (extract)
100 g/3^1/$_2$ oz/7 tbsp caster
  (superfine) sugar
100 g/3^1/$_2$ oz/generous ^{1}/$_3$ cup butter

150 g/5^1/$_2$ oz/1^1/$_4$ cups self-raising
  flour
2 tbsp cocoa powder
icing (confectioners') sugar, to dust

FOR THE SAUCE:
3 tbsp cocoa powder
50 g/1^3/$_4$ oz/4 tbsp light muscovado
  sugar
300 ml/^{1}/$_2$ pint/1^1/$_4$ cups boiling
  water

1 Lightly grease an 850 ml\1^1/$_2$ pint/3^3/$_4$ cup ovenproof dish.

2 Place the milk in a small pan. Break the chocolate into pieces and add to the milk. Heat gently, stirring until the chocolate melts. Leave to cool slightly. Stir in the vanilla flavouring (extract).

3 Beat together the caster (superfine) sugar and butter in a bowl until light and fluffy. Sieve (strain) the flour and cocoa powder together. Add to the bowl with the chocolate milk and beat until smooth, using an electric whisk if you have one. Pour the mixture into the prepared dish.

4 To make the sauce, mix together the cocoa powder and sugar. Add a little boiling water and mix to a smooth paste, then stir in the remaining water. Pour the sauce over the pudding but do not mix in.

5 Place the dish on to a baking tray (cookie sheet) and bake in a preheated oven, 180°C/350°F/Gas Mark 4, for 40 minutes or until dry on top and springy to the touch. Leave to stand for about 5 minutes, then dust with a little icing (confectioners') sugar just before serving.

VARIATION

For a mocha sauce, add 1 tbsp instant coffee to the cocoa powder and sugar in step 4, before mixing to a paste with the boiling water.

Pecan & Chocolate Fudge Ring

Although this can be served cold as a cake, it is absolutely delicious served hot as a pudding.

Serves 6

INGREDIENTS

FUDGE SAUCE:
40 g/1^1/$_2$ oz/3 tbsp butter
40 g/1^1/$_2$ oz/3 tbsp light muscovado
   sugar
4 tbsp golden (light corn) syrup
2 tbsp milk
1 tbsp cocoa powder

40 g/1^1/$_2$ oz dark chocolate
50 g/1^3/$_4$ oz pecan nuts, finely
   chopped

CAKE:
100 g/3^1/$_2$ oz/generous ^{1}/$_3$ cup soft
   margarine

100 g/3^1/$_2$ oz/7 tbsp light muscovado
   sugar
125 g/4^1/$_2$ oz/1 cup self-raising flour
2 eggs
2 tbsp milk
1 tbsp golden (light corn) syrup

1 Lightly grease a 20 cm/8 inch ring tin (pan).

2 To make the fudge sauce, place the butter, sugar, syrup, milk and cocoa powder in a small pan and heat gently, stirring until combined.

3 Break the chocolate into pieces, add to the mixture and stir until melted. Stir in the chopped nuts. Pour into the base of the tin (pan) and leave to cool.

4 To make the cake, place all of the ingredients in a mixing bowl and beat until smooth. Carefully spoon the cake mixture over the chocolate fudge sauce.

5 Bake in a preheated oven, 180°C/350°F/Gas Mark 4, for 35 minutes or until the cake is springy to the touch.

6 Leave to cool in the tin (pan) for 5 minutes, then turn out on to a serving dish and serve.

COOK'S TIP

To make in the microwave, place the butter, sugar, syrup, milk and cocoa powder for the sauce in a microwave-proof bowl. Cook on High for 2 minutes, stirring twice. Stir in the chocolate until melted, then add the nuts. Pour into a 1.1 litre/2 pint/ 5 cup microwave-proof ring mould (mold). Make the cake and cook on High for 3-4 minutes until just dry on top; stand for 5 minutes.

Chocolate Meringue Pie

Crumbly biscuit base, rich creamy chocolate filling topped with fluffy meringue – what could be more indulgent than this fabulous dessert?

Serves 6

INGREDIENTS

225 g/8 oz dark chocolate digestive
   biscuits (graham crackers)
50 g/1³/4 oz/4 tbsp butter

FILLING:
3 egg yolks

50 g/1³/4 oz/4 tbsp caster (superfine)
   sugar
4 tbsp cornflour (cornstarch)
600 ml/1 pint/2¹/2 cups milk
100 g/3¹/2 oz dark chocolate, melted

MERINGUE:
2 egg whites
100 g/3¹/2 oz/7 tbsp caster
   (superfine) sugar
¹/4 tsp vanilla flavouring (extract)

1 Place the digestive biscuits (graham crackers) in a plastic bag and crush with a rolling pin. Pour into a mixing bowl. Melt the butter and stir it into the biscuit (cracker) crumbs until well mixed. Press the biscuit mixture firmly into the base and up the sides of a 23 cm/9 inch flan tin (pan) or dish.

2 To make the filling, beat the egg yolks, caster (superfine) sugar and cornflour (cornstarch) in a large bowl until they form a smooth paste, adding a little of the milk if necessary. Heat the milk until almost boiling, then slowly pour it on to the egg mixture, whisking well.

3 Return the mixture to the saucepan and cook gently, whisking constantly until it thickens. Remove from the heat. Whisk in the melted chocolate, then pour it on to the digestive biscuit (graham cracker) base.

4 To make the meringue, whisk the egg whites in a large mixing bowl until standing in soft peaks. Gradually whisk in about two-thirds of the sugar until the mixture is stiff and glossy. Fold in the remaining sugar and vanilla flavouring (extract).

5 Spread the meringue over the filling, swirling the surface with the back of a spoon to give it an attractive finish. Bake in the centre of a preheated oven, 170°C/375°F/Gas Mark 3, for 30 minutes or until the meringue is golden. Serve hot or just warm.

Chocolate Apple Pie

Easy-to-make crumbly chocolate pastry encases a delicious apple filling studded with chocolate chips. This recipe is guaranteed to become a firm family favourite.

Serves 6

INGREDIENTS

CHOCOLATE PASTRY:
4 tbsp cocoa powder
200 g/7 oz/1^3/4 cups plain (all-purpose) flour
2 egg yolks
100 g/3^1/2 oz/^{3}/4 cup softened butter
50 g/1^3/4 oz/4 tbsp caster (superfine) sugar

few drops of vanilla flavouring (extract)
cold water, to mix

FILLING:
750 g/1 lb 10 oz cooking apples
25 g/1 oz/2 tbsp butter
^{1}/2 tsp ground cinnamon

50 g/1^3/4 oz/^{3}/4 cup dark chocolate chips
a little egg white, beaten
^{1}/2 tsp caster (superfine) sugar
whipped cream or vanilla ice cream, to serve

1 To make the pastry, sieve (strain) the cocoa powder and flour into a mixing bowl and rub in the butter until the mixture resembles fine breadcrumbs. Stir in the sugar. Add the egg yolk, vanilla flavouring (extract) and enough water to mix to a dough.

2 Roll out the dough on a lightly floured surface and use to line a deep 20 cm/8 inch flan or cake tin (pan). Chill for 30 minutes. Roll out any trimmings and cut out some pastry leaves to decorate the top of the pie.

3 Peel, core and thickly slice the apples. Place half of the apple slices in a saucepan with the butter and cinnamon and cook over a gently heat, stirring occasionally until the apples soften.

4 Stir in the uncooked apple slices, leave to cool slightly, then stir in the chocolate chips. Prick the base of the pastry case (pie shell) and pile the apple mixture into it. Arrange the pastry leaves on top. Brush the leaves with a little egg white and sprinkle with caster (superfine) sugar.

5 Bake in a preheated oven, 180°C/350°F/Gas Mark 4, for 35 minutes until the pastry is crisp. Serve warm or cold, with whipped cream or vanilla ice cream.

Chocolate Pear & Almond Flan

This attractive dessert consists of a flan filled with pears cooked in a chocolate, almond-flavoured sponge. It is delicious served hot or cold.

Serves 6

INGREDIENTS

100 g/3¹/₂ oz/³/₄ cup plain (all-purpose) flour
25 g/1 oz/¹/₄ cup ground almonds
60 g/2 oz/¹/₄ cup block margarine
about 3 tbsp water

FILLING:
400 g/14 oz can pear halves, in natural juice
50 g/1³/₄ oz/4 tbsp butter

50 g/1³/₄ oz/4 tbsp caster (superfine) sugar
2 eggs, beaten
100 g/3¹/₂ oz/1 cup ground almonds
2 tbsp cocoa powder
few drops of almond flavouring (extract)
icing (confectioners') sugar, to dust

CHOCOLATE SAUCE:
50 g/1³/₄ oz/4 tbsp caster (superfine) sugar
3 tbsp golden (light corn) syrup
100 ml/3 fl oz/¹/₃ cup water
175 g/6 oz dark chocolate, broken into pieces
25 g/1 oz/2 tbsp butter

1 Lightly grease a 20 cm/8 inch flan tin (pan). Sieve (strain) the flour into a mixing bowl and stir in the almonds. Rub in the margarine with your fingertips until the mixture resembles breadcrumbs. Add enough water to mix to a soft dough. Cover, chill in the freezer for 10 minutes, then roll out and use to line the tin (pan). Prick the base and chill.

2 To make the filling, drain the pears well. Beat the butter and sugar until light and fluffy. Beat in the eggs. Fold in the almonds, cocoa powder and flavouring (extract). Spread the chocolate mixture in the pastry case (pie shell) and arrange the pears on top, pressing down lightly. Bake in the centre of a preheated oven, 200°C/400°F/Gas Mark 6, for 30 minutes

or until the filling has risen. Cool slightly and transfer to a serving dish, if wished. Dust with sugar.

3 To make the sauce, place the sugar, syrup and water in a pan and heat gently, stirring until the sugar dissolves. Boil gently for 1 minute. Remove from the heat, add the chocolate and butter and stir until melted. Serve with the flan.

Chocolate & Banana Pancakes

Pancakes are given the chocolate treatment to make a rich and fabulous dessert to round off a dinner party. Prepare this recipe ahead of time for trouble-free entertaining.

Serves 4

INGREDIENTS

3 large bananas
6 tbsp orange juice
grated rind of 1 orange
2 tbsp orange- or banana-flavoured
  liqueur

HOT CHOCOLATE SAUCE:
1 tbsp cocoa powder

2 tsp cornflour (cornstarch)
3 tbsp milk
40 g/1^1/$_2$ oz dark chocolate
15 g/^{1}/$_2$ oz/1 tbsp butter
175 g/6 oz/^{1}/$_2$ cup golden (light corn)
  syrup
^{1}/$_4$ tsp vanilla flavouring (extract)

PANCAKES:
100 g/3^1/$_2$ oz/1 cup plain (all-
  purpose) flour
1 tbsp cocoa powder
1 egg
1 tsp sunflower oil
300 ml/^{1}/$_2$ pint/1^1/$_4$ cups milk
oil, for frying

1 Peel and slice the bananas and arrange them in a dish with the orange juice and rind and the liqueur. Set aside.

2 Mix the cocoa powder and cornflour (cornstarch) in a bowl, then stir in the milk. Break the dark chocolate into pieces and place in a pan with the butter and golden (light corn) syrup. Heat gently, stirring until well blended. Add the cocoa mixture and bring to the boil over a gentle heat, stirring. Simmer for 1 minute, then remove from the heat and stir in the vanilla flavouring (extract).

3 To make the pancakes, sieve (strain) the flour and cocoa into a mixing bowl and make a well in the centre. Add the egg and oil. Gradually whisk in the milk to form a smooth batter. Heat a little oil in a heavy-based frying pan (skillet) and pour off any excess. Pour in a little batter and tilt the pan to coat the base. Cook over a medium heat until the underside is browned. Flip over and cook the other side. Slide the pancake out of the pan and keep warm. Repeat until all the batter has been used.

4 To serve, reheat the chocolate sauce for 1-2 minutes. Fill the pancakes with the bananas and fold in half or into triangles. Pour over a little chocolate sauce and serve.

Chocolate Apple Pancake Stack

If you cannot wait to get your first chocolate 'fix' of the day, serve these pancakes for breakfast. They also make a perfect family dessert.

Serves 4–6

INGREDIENTS

225 g/8 oz/2 cups plain (all-purpose) flour
1^1/$_2$ tsp baking powder
50 g/1^3/$_4$ oz/4 tbsp caster (superfine) sugar

1 egg
1 tbsp butter, melted
300 ml/^{1}/$_2$ pint/1^1/$_4$ cups milk
1 eating apple
50 g/1^3/$_4$ oz dark chocolate chips

Hot Chocolate Sauce (see page 160) or maple syrup, to serve

1 Sieve (strain) the flour and baking powder into a mixing bowl. Stir in the caster (superfine) sugar. Make a well in the centre and add the egg and melted butter. Gradually whisk in the milk to form a smooth batter.

2 Peel, core and grate the apple and stir it into the batter with the chocolate chips.

3 Heat a griddle or heavy-based frying pan (skillet) over a medium heat and grease it lightly. For each pancake, place about 2 tablespoons of the batter on to the griddle or pan (skillet) and spread to make a 7.5 cm/3 inch round.

4 Cook for a few minutes until you see bubbles appear on the surface of the pancake. Turn over and cook for a further 1 minute. Remove from the pan and keep warm. Repeat with the remaining batter to make about 12 pancakes.

5 To serve, stack 2 or 3 pancakes on an individual serving plate and serve with the hot chocolate sauce or maple syrup.

COOK'S TIP

To keep the cooked pancakes warm, pile them on top of each other with baking parchment in between to prevent them sticking to each other.

VARIATION

Milk chocolate chips can be used instead of the dark ones, if preferred.

Chocolate Fondue

This is a fun dessert to serve at the end of the meal. Prepare
in advance, then just warm through before serving.

Serves 6–8

INGREDIENTS

CHOCOLATE FONDUE:
225 g/8 oz dark chocolate

200 ml/7 fl oz/$^{3}/_{4}$ cup double (heavy)
cream
2 tbsp brandy

TO SERVE:
selection of fruit
white and pink marshmallows
sweet biscuits (cookies)

1 Break the chocolate into small pieces and place in a small saucepan with the double (heavy) cream.

2 Heat the mixture gently, stirring constantly until the chocolate has melted and blended with the cream.

3 Remove the pan from the heat and stir in the brandy.

4 Pour into a fondue pot or a small flameproof dish and keep warm, preferably over a small burner.

5 Serve with a selection of fruit, marshmallows and biscuits (cookies) for dipping. The fruit and marshmallows can be spiked on fondue forks, wooden skewers or ordinary forks for dipping into the chocolate fondue.

COOK'S TIP

To prepare the fruit for dipping, cut larger fruit into bite-size pieces. Fruit which discolours, such as bananas, apples and pears, should be dipped in a little lemon juice as soon as it is cut.

COOK'S TIP

It is not essential to use a special fondue set. Dish warmers which use a night light are just as good for keeping the fondue warm. If you do not have one, stand the fondue dish in a larger dish and pour in enough boiling water to come halfway up the fondue dish. Whichever method you use to keep your fondue warm, place it on a heatproof stand to protect the table.

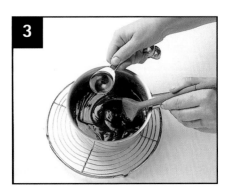

Hot Chocolate Soufflé

Served with hot chocolate custard this is a chocoholic's dream come true. Do not be put off by the mystique of soufflés – this one really is not at all difficult to make.

Serves 4

INGREDIENTS

100 g/3^1/2 oz dark chocolate
300 ml/^{1}/2 pint/1^1/4 cups milk
25 g/1 oz/2 tbsp butter
4 large eggs, separated
1 tbsp cornflour (cornstarch)
50 g/1^3/4 oz/4 tbsp caster (superfine)
  sugar

^{1}/2 tsp vanilla flavouring (extract)
100 g/3^1/2 oz/^{2}/3 cup dark chocolate
  chips
caster (superfine) and icing
  (confectioners') sugar, to dust

CHOCOLATE CUSTARD:
2 tbsp cornflour (cornstarch)
1 tbsp caster (superfine) sugar
450 ml/^{3}/4 pint/2 cups milk
50 g/1^3/4 oz dark chocolate

1 Grease an 850 ml/1^1/2 pint/
5 cup soufflé dish and sprinkle with caster (superfine) sugar. Break the chocolate into pieces.

2 Heat the milk with the butter in a pan until almost boiling. Mix the egg yolks, cornflour (cornstarch) and caster (superfine) sugar in a bowl and pour on some of the hot milk, whisking. Return it to the pan and cook gently, stirring constantly until thickened. Add the chocolate and stir until

melted. Remove from the heat and stir in the flavouring (extract).

3 Whisk the egg whites until standing in soft peaks. Fold half of the egg whites into the chocolate mixture. Fold in the rest with the chocolate chips. Pour into the dish and bake in a preheated oven, 180°C/350°F/Gas Mark 4, for 40-45 minutes until well risen.

4 Meanwhile, make the custard. Put the cornflour (cornstarch)

and sugar in a small bowl and mix to a smooth paste with a little of the milk. Heat the remaining milk until almost boiling. Pour a little of the hot milk on to the cornflour (cornstarch), mix well, then pour back into the pan. Cook gently, stirring until thickened. Break the chocolate into pieces and add to the custard, stirring until melted.

5 Dust the soufflé with sugar and serve immediately with the chocolate custard.

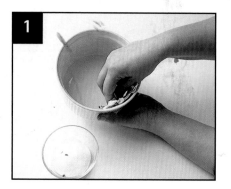

Chocolate Zabaglione

As light as air with a creamy texture, this sophisticated dessert is sure to be a real winner. As it only uses a little chocolate, choose one with a minimum of 70 per cent cocoa solids for a good flavour.

Serves 2

INGREDIENTS

4 egg yolks
50 g/1³/₄ oz/4 tbsp caster (superfine) sugar

50 g/1³/₄ oz dark chocolate
125 ml/4 fl oz/1 cup Marsala wine

cocoa powder, to dust

1 In a large glass mixing bowl, whisk together the egg yolks and caster (superfine) sugar until you have a very pale mixture, using electric beaters.

2 Grate the chocolate finely and fold into the egg mixture. Fold in the wine.

3 Place the mixing bowl over a saucepan of gently simmering water and set the beaters on the lowest speed or swop to a balloon whisk. Cook gently, whisking continuously until the mixture thickens; take care not to overcook or the mixture will curdle.

4 Spoon the hot mixture into warmed individual glass dishes and dust lightly with cocoa powder. Serve the zabaglione as soon as possible so that it is warm, light and fluffy.

COOK'S TIP

Make the dessert just before serving as the mixture will separate if left to stand. If it begins to curdle, you may be able to save it if you remove it from the heat immediately and place it in a bowl of cold water to stop the cooking. Whisk furiously until the mixture comes together.

COOK'S TIP

For an up-to-the minute serving idea, spoon the zabaglione into coffee cups and serve with amaretti biscuits to the side of the saucer.

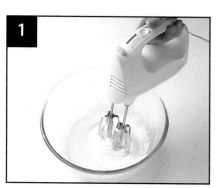

Cold Desserts

*Cool, creamy, sumptuous, indulgent
are just a few of the words that spring to mind
when you think of cold chocolate desserts.
The desserts contained in this chapter are a
combination of all of these.*

*Some of the desserts are surprisingly quick
and simple to make, while others are more elaborate.
One of the best things about these desserts is they can
all be made in advance, some times days in advance,
making them perfect for entertaining. A quick
decoration when necessary is all that is needed on
the day. Even the Baked Chocolate Alaska can be
assembled in advance and popped into the
oven just before serving.*

Chocolate Mint Swirl

*The classic combination of chocolate and mint flavours makes
an attractive dessert for special occasions.*

Serves 6

INGREDIENTS

300 ml/^{1}/$_2$ pint/1^1/$_4$ cups double
(heavy) cream
150 ml/^{1}/$_4$ pint/^{2}/$_3$ cup creamy
fromage frais

25 g/1 oz/2 tbsp icing (confectioners')
sugar
1 tbsp crème de menthe
175 g/6 oz dark chocolate

chocolate, to decorate

1 Place the cream in a large mixing bowl and whisk until standing in soft peaks.

2 Fold in the fromage frais and icing (confectioners') sugar, then place about one-third of the mixture in a smaller bowl. Stir the crème de menthe into the smaller bowl. Melt the dark chocolate and stir it into the remaining mixture.

3 Place alternate spoonfuls of the 2 mixtures into serving glasses, then swirl the mixture together to give a decorative effect. Leave to chill until required.

4 To make the piped chocolate decorations, melt a small amount of chocolate and place in a paper piping bag.

5 Place a sheet of baking parchment on a board and pipe squiggles, stars or flower shapes with the melted chocolate. Alternatively, to make curved decorations, pipe decorations on to a long strip of baking parchment, then carefully place the strip over a rolling pin, securing with sticky tape. Leave the chocolate to set, then carefully remove from the baking parchment.

6 Decorate each dessert with piped chocolate decorations and serve. The desserts can be decorated and then chilled, if preferred.

COOK'S TIP

*Pipe the patterns freehand or draw
patterns on to baking parchment
first, turn the parchment over
and then pipe the chocolate,
following the drawn outline.*

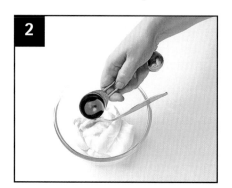

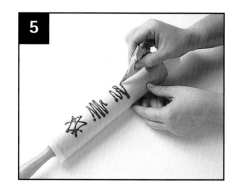

Chocolate Rum Pots

*Wickedly rich little pots, flavoured with a hint
of dark rum, for pure indulgence!*

Serves 6

INGREDIENTS

225 g/8 oz dark chocolate
4 eggs, separated
75 g/2^3/4 oz/^{1}/3 cup caster
(superfine) sugar

4 tbsp dark rum
4 tbsp double (heavy) cream

TO DECORATE:
a little whipped cream
chocolate shapes (see page 176)

1 Melt the chocolate and leave to cool slightly.

2 Whisk the egg yolks with the caster (superfine) sugar in a bowl until very pale and fluffy; this will take about 5 minutes with electric beaters, a little longer with a balloon whisk.

3 Drizzle the chocolate into the mixture and fold in together with the rum and the double (heavy) cream.

4 Whisk the egg whites in a grease-free bowl until standing in soft peaks. Fold the egg whites into the chocolate mixture in 2 batches. Divide the mixture between 6 ramekins (custard pots), or other individual dishes, and leave to chill for at least 2 hours.

5 To serve, decorate with a little whipped cream and small chocolate shapes.

VARIATION

These delicious little pots can be flavoured with brandy instead of rum, if preferred.

COOK'S TIP

Make sure you use a perfectly clean and grease-free bowl for whisking the egg whites. They will not aerate if any grease is present as the smallest amount breaks down the bubbles in the whites, preventing them from trapping and holding air.

Chocolate & Vanilla Creams

These rich, creamy desserts are completely irresistible.
Serve them with crisp dessert biscuits (cookies).

Serves 4

INGREDIENTS

450 ml/16 fl oz/2 cups double (heavy) cream
75 g/2¾ oz/⅓ cup caster (superfine) sugar
1 vanilla pod

200 ml/7 fl oz/¾ cup crème fraîche
2 tsp gelatine
3 tbsp water
50 g/1¾ oz dark chocolate

MARBLED CHOCOLATE SHAPES:
a little melted white chocolate
a little melted dark chocolate

1 Place the cream and sugar in a saucepan. Cut the vanilla pod into 2 pieces and add to the cream. Heat gently, stirring until the sugar has dissolved, then bring to the boil. Reduce the heat and leave to simmer for 2-3 minutes.

2 Remove the pan from the heat and take out the vanilla pod. Stir in the crème fraîche.

3 Sprinkle the gelatine over the water in a small heatproof bowl and leave to go spongy, then place over a pan of hot water and stir until dissolved. Stir into the cream mixture. Pour half of this mixture into another mixing bowl.

4 Melt the dark chocolate and stir it into one half of the cream mixture. Pour the chocolate mixture into 4 individual glass serving dishes and chill for 15-20 minutes until just set. While it is chilling, keep the vanilla mixture at room temperature.

5 Spoon the vanilla mixture on top of the chocolate mixture and chill until the vanilla is set.

6 Meanwhile, make the shapes for the decoration. Spoon the melted white chocolate into a paper piping bag and snip off the tip. Spread some melted dark chocolate on a piece of baking parchment. Whilst still wet, pipe a fine line of white chocolate in a scribble over the top. Use the tip of a cocktail stick (toothpick) to marble the white chocolate into the dark. When firm but not too hard, cut into shapes with a small shaped cutter or a sharp knife. Chill the shapes until firm, then use to decorate the desserts.

Chocolate Hazelnut Pots

Chocoholics will adore these creamy desserts consisting of a rich baked chocolate custard with the delicious flavour of hazelnuts.

Serves 6

INGREDIENTS

2 eggs
2 egg yolks
15 g/$^1/_2$ oz/1 tbsp caster (superfine) sugar

1 tsp cornflour (cornstarch)
600 ml/1 pint/2$^1/_2$ cups milk
75 g/3 oz dark chocolate
4 tbsp chocolate and hazelnut spread

TO DECORATE:
grated chocolate or large chocolate curls (see page 66)

1 Beat together the eggs, egg yolks, caster (superfine) sugar and cornflour (cornstarch) until well combined. Heat the milk until almost boiling.

2 Gradually pour the milk on to the eggs, whisking as you do so. Melt the chocolate and hazelnut spread in a bowl set over a pan of gently simmering water, then whisk the melted chocolate mixture into the eggs.

3 Pour into 6 small ovenproof dishes and cover the dishes with foil. Place them in a roasting tin (pan). Fill the tin (pan) with boiling water to come halfway up the sides of the dishes.

4 Bake in a preheated oven, 170°C/325°F/Gas Mark 3, for 35-40 minutes until the custard is just set. Remove from the tin (pan) and cool, then chill until required. Serve decorated with grated chocolate or chocolate curls.

COOK'S TIP

The foil lid prevents a skin forming on the surface of the custards.

COOK'S TIP

This dish is traditionally made in little pots called pots de crème, *which are individual ovenproof dishes with a lid. Ramekins (custard pots) are fine. The dessert can also be made in one large dish; cook for about 1 hour or until set.*

Mocha Creams

These creamy chocolate and coffee-flavoured desserts
make a perfect end to a fine meal.

Serves 4

INGREDIENTS

225 g/8 oz dark chocolate
1 tbsp instant coffee
300 ml/^{1}/$_2$ pint/1^1/$_4$ cups boiling
   water
1 sachet (envelope) gelatine

3 tbsp cold water
1 tsp vanilla flavouring (extract)
1 tbsp coffee-flavoured liqueur
   (optional)

300 ml/^{1}/$_2$ pint/1^1/$_4$ cups double
   (heavy) cream
4 chocolate coffee beans
8 amaretti biscuits (cookies)

1 Break the chocolate into small pieces and place in a saucepan with the coffee. Stir in the boiling water and heat gently, stirring until the chocolate melts.

2 Sprinkle the gelatine over the cold water and leave to go spongy, then whisk it into the hot chocolate mixture to dissolve it.

3 Stir in the vanilla flavouring (extract) and coffee-flavoured liqueur, if using. Leave to stand in a cool place until just beginning to thicken; whisk from time to time.

4 Whisk the cream until it is standing in soft peaks, then reserve a little for decorating the desserts and fold the remainder into the chocolate mixture. Spoon into serving dishes and leave to set.

5 Decorate with the reserved cream and coffee beans and serve with the biscuits (cookies).

COOK'S TIP

If preferred, the puddings can be made in one large serving dish.

VARIATION

To add a delicious almond flavour to the dessert, replace the coffee-flavoured liqueur with almond-flavoured (amaretto) liqueur.

Layered Chocolate Mousse

Three layers of fabulous rich mousse give this elegant dessert extra chocolate appeal. It is a little fiddly to prepare, but well worth the extra effort.

Serves 8

INGREDIENTS

3 eggs
1 tsp cornflour (cornstarch)
50 g/1^3/$_4$ oz/4 tbsp caster (superfine) sugar
300 ml/^{1}/$_2$ pint/1^1/$_4$ cups milk

1 sachet (envelope) gelatine
3 tbsp water
300 ml/^{1}/$_2$ pint/1^1/$_4$ cups double (heavy) cream
75 g/2^3/$_4$ oz dark chocolate

75 g/2^3/$_4$ oz white chocolate
75 g/2^3/$_4$ oz milk chocolate
chocolate caraque, to decorate (see page 208)

1 Line a 450 g/1 lb loaf tin (pan) with baking parchment. Separate the eggs, putting each egg white in a separate bowl. Place the egg yolks and sugar in a large mixing bowl and whisk until well combined. Place the milk in a pan and heat gently, stirring until almost boiling. Pour the milk on to the egg yolks, whisking.

2 Set the bowl over a pan of gently simmering water and cook, stirring until the mixture thickens enough to thinly coat the back of a wooden spoon.

3 Sprinkle the gelatine over the water in a small heatproof bowl and leave to go spongy. Place over a pan of hot water and stir until dissolved. Stir into the hot mixture. Leave to cool.

4 Whip the cream until just holding its shape. Fold into the egg custard, then divide the mixture into 3. Melt the 3 types of chocolate separately. Fold the dark chocolate into one egg custard portion. Whisk one egg white until standing in soft peaks and fold into the dark chocolate custard until

combined. Pour into the prepared tin (pan) and level the top. Chill in the coldest part of the refrigerator until just set. Leave the remaining mixtures at room temperature.

5 Fold the white chocolate into another portion of the egg custard. Whisk another egg white and fold in. Pour on top of the dark chocolate layer and chill quickly. Repeat with the remaining milk chocolate and egg white. Chill until set. To serve, carefully turn out on to a serving dish and decorate with chocolate caraque.

Chocolate Marquise

This is a classic French dish, part way between a mousse and parfait. It is usually chilled in a large mould (mold), but here it is served in individual moulds (molds).

Serves 6

INGREDIENTS

200 g/7 oz dark chocolate
100 g/3^1/2 oz/generous ^{1}/3 cup butter
3 egg yolks
75 g/2^3/4 oz/^{1}/3 cup caster
    (superfine) sugar

1 tsp chocolate flavouring (extract)
    or 1 tbsp chocolate-flavoured
    liqueur
300 ml/^{1}/2 pint/1^1/4 cups double
    (heavy) cream

TO SERVE:
crème fraîche
chocolate-dipped fruits (see page 64)
cocoa powder, to dust

1 Break the chocolate into pieces. Place the chocolate and butter in a bowl over a pan of gently simmering water and stir until melted and well combined. Remove from the heat and leave to cool.

2 Place the egg yolks in a mixing bowl with the sugar and whisk until pale and fluffy. Using an electric whisk running on low speed, slowly whisk in the cool chocolate mixture. Stir in the chocolate flavouring (extract) or chocolate-flavoured liqueur.

3 Whip the cream until just holding its shape. Fold into the chocolate mixture. Spoon into 6 small ramekins (custard pots), or individual metal moulds (molds). Leave to chill for at least 2 hours.

4 To serve, turn out the desserts on to individual serving dishes. If you have difficulty turning them out, dip the moulds (molds) into a bowl of warm water for a few seconds to help the marquise to slip out. Serve with chocolate-dipped fruit and crème fraîche and dust with cocoa powder.

COOK'S TIP

The slight tartness of the crème fraîche contrasts well with this very rich dessert. Dip the fruit in white chocolate to give a good colour contrast.

Iced White Chocolate Terrine

This iced dessert is somewhere between a chocolate mousse and an ice cream.
Serve it with a chocolate sauce or a fruit coulis and fresh fruit.

Serves 8-10

INGREDIENTS

2 tbsp granulated sugar
5 tbsp water

300 g/10^1/$_2$ oz white chocolate
3 eggs, separated

300 ml/^{1}/$_2$ pint/1^1/$_4$ cups double
(heavy) cream

1 Line a 450 g/1 lb loaf tin (pan) with foil or cling film (plastic wrap), pressing out as many creases as you can.

2 Place the granulated sugar and water in a heavy-based pan and heat gently, stirring until the sugar has dissolved. Bring to the boil and boil for 1-2 minutes until syrupy, then remove the pan from the heat.

3 Break the white chocolate into small pieces and stir it into the syrup, continuing to stir until the chocolate has melted and combined with the syrup. Leave to cool slightly.

4 Beat the egg yolks into the chocolate mixture. Leave to cool completely.

5 Lightly whip the cream until just holding its shape and fold it into the chocolate mixture.

6 Whisk the egg whites in a grease-free bowl until they are standing in soft peaks. Fold into the chocolate mixture. Pour into the prepared loaf tin (pan) and freeze overnight.

7 To serve, remove from the freezer about 10-15 minutes before serving. Turn out of the tin (pan) and cut into slices to serve.

COOK'S TIP

To make a coulis, place 225 g/8 oz soft fruit of your choice – strawberries, black or red currants, mango or raspberries are ideal – in a food processor or blender. Add 1-2 tbsp icing (confectioners') sugar and blend to form a purée. If the fruit contains seeds, push the purée through a sieve to remove them. Leave to chill until required.

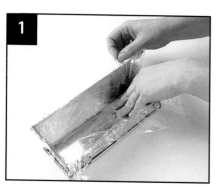

Chocolate Banana Sundae

*A banana split in a glass! Choose the best vanilla ice cream
you can find, or better still make you own.*

Serves 4

INGREDIENTS

GLOSSY CHOCOLATE SAUCE:
60 g/2 oz dark chocolate
4 tbsp golden (light corn) syrup
15 g/^{1}/$_2$ oz/1 tbsp butter
1 tbsp brandy or rum (optional)

SUNDAE:
4 bananas
150 ml/^{1}/$_4$ pint/^{2}/$_3$ cup double
  (heavy) cream
8-12 scoops of good quality vanilla
  ice cream

75 g/2^3/$_4$ oz/^{2}/$_3$ cup flaked (slivered)
  or chopped almonds, toasted
grated or flaked chocolate, to
  sprinkle
4 fan wafer biscuits (cookies)

1 To make the chocolate sauce, break the chocolate into small pieces and place in a heatproof bowl with the syrup and butter. Heat over a pan of hot water until melted, stirring until well combined. Remove the bowl from the heat and stir in the brandy or rum, if using.

2 Slice the bananas and whip the cream until just holding its shape. Place a scoop of ice cream in the bottom of 4 tall sundae dishes. Top with slices of banana, some chocolate sauce, a spoonful of cream and a good sprinkling of nuts.

3 Repeat the layers, finishing with a good dollop of cream, sprinkled with nuts and a little grated or flaked chocolate. Serve with fan wafer biscuits (cookies).

VARIATION

Use half vanilla ice cream and half chocolate ice cream, if you like.

VARIATION

For a traditional banana split, halve the bananas lengthways and place on a plate with two scoops of ice cream between. Top with cream and sprinkle with nuts. Serve with the glossy chocolate sauce poured over the top.

Rich Chocolate Ice Cream

A rich flavoured chocolate ice cream which is delicious served on its own or with a chocolate sauce. For a special dessert, serve in these attractive trellis cups.

Serves 6-8

INGREDIENTS

ICE CREAM:
1 egg
3 egg yolks
90 g/3 oz/6 tbsp caster (superfine) sugar

300 ml/^{1}/2 pint/1^1/4 cups full cream milk
250 g/9 oz dark chocolate
300 ml/^{1}/2 pint/1^1/4 cups double (heavy) cream

TRELLIS CUPS:
100 g/3^1/2 oz dark chocolate

1 Beat together the egg, egg yolks and caster (superfine) sugar in a mixing bowl until well combined. Heat the milk until almost boiling.

2 Gradually pour the hot milk on to the eggs, whisking as you do so. Place the bowl over a pan of gently simmering water and cook, stirring until the mixture thickens sufficiently to thinly coat the back of a wooden spoon.

3 Break the dark chocolate into small pieces and add to the hot custard. Stir until the chocolate has melted. Cover with a sheet of dampened baking parchment and leave to cool.

4 Whip the cream until just holding its shape, then fold into the cooled chocolate custard. Transfer to a freezer container and freeze for 1-2 hours until the mixture is frozen 2.5 cm/1 inch from the sides.

5 Scrape the ice cream into a chilled bowl and beat again until smooth. Re-freeze until firm.

6 To make the trellis cups, invert a muffin tray (pan) and cover 6 alternate mounds with cling film (plastic wrap). Melt the chocolate, place it in a paper piping bag and snip off the end.

7 Pipe a circle around the base of the mound, then pipe chocolate back and forth over it to form a trellis; carefully pipe a double thickness. Pipe around the base again. Chill until set, then lift from the tray (pan) and remove the cling film (plastic wrap). Serve the ice cream in the trellis cups.

Baked Chocolate Alaska

A cool dessert that leaves the cook completely unflustered. Light meringue tops chocolate ice cream for this divine dessert – you can assemble it in advance and pop into the freezer until required.

Serves 6

INGREDIENTS

2 eggs
50 g/1³/4 oz/4 tbsp caster (superfine) sugar
40 g/1¹/2 oz/generous ¹/4 cup plain (all-purpose) flour

15 g/¹/2 oz/2 tbsp cocoa powder
3 egg whites
150 g/5¹/2 oz/²/3 cup caster (superfine) sugar

1 litre/1³/4 pint/4¹/2 cups good quality chocolate ice cream

1 Grease an 18 cm/7 inch round cake tin (pan) and line the base with baking parchment.

2 Whisk the egg and the 4 tbsp sugar in a mixing bowl until very thick and pale. Sieve (strain) the flour and cocoa powder together and carefully fold in.

3 Pour into the prepared tin (pan) and bake in a preheated oven, 220°C/425°F/Gas Mark 7, for 7 minutes or until springy to the touch. Transfer to a wire rack to cool completely.

4 Whisk the egg whites in a grease-free bowl until they are standing in soft peaks. Gradually add the sugar, whisking until you have a thick, glossy meringue.

5 Place the sponge on a baking tray (cookie sheet) and pile the ice cream on to the centre in a heaped dome.

6 Pipe or spread the meringue over the ice cream, making sure the ice cream is completely enclosed. (At this point the dessert can be frozen, if wished.)

7 Return it to the oven, for 5 minutes until the meringue is just golden. Serve immediately.

COOK'S TIP

This dessert is delicious served with a blackcurrant coulis. Cook a few blackcurrants in a little orange juice until soft, purée and push through a sieve, then sweeten to taste with a little icing (confectioners') sugar.

White Chocolate Ice Cream in a Biscuit (Cookie) Cup

This white chocolate ice cream is served in a biscuit (cookie) cup.
If liked, top with a chocolate sauce for a true addict's treat.

Serves 6

INGREDIENTS

ICE CREAM:
1 egg
1 egg yolk
40 g/1½ oz/3 tbsp caster (superfine)
  sugar
150 g/5½ oz white chocolate
300 ml/½ pint/1¼ cups milk

150 ml/¼ pint/⅔ cup double
  (heavy) cream

BISCUIT (COOKIE) CUPS:
1 egg white
50 g/1¾ oz/4 tbsp caster (superfine)
  sugar

15 g/½ oz/2 tbsp plain (all-purpose)
  flour, sieved (strained)
15 g/½ oz/2 tbsp cocoa powder,
  sieved (strained)
25 g/1 oz/2 tbsp butter, melted

1 Place baking parchment on 2 baking trays (cookie sheets). To make the ice cream, beat the egg, egg yolks and sugar. Break the chocolate into pieces, place in a bowl with 3 tbsp milk and melt over a pan of hot water. Heat the milk until almost boiling and pour on to the eggs, whisking. Place over a pan of simmering water and cook, stirring until the mixture thickens enough to coat the back of a wooden spoon. Whisk in the chocolate. Cover with dampened baking parchment and let cool.

2 Whip the cream until just holding its shape and fold into the custard. Transfer to a freezer container and freeze the mixture for 1-2 hours until frozen 2.5 cm/ 1 inch from the sides. Scrape into a bowl and beat again until smooth. Re-freeze until firm.

3 To make the cups, beat the egg white and sugar together. Beat in the flour and cocoa, then the butter. Place 1 tbsp of mixture on one tray (sheet); spread out to a 12.5 cm/5 inch circle. Bake in a preheated oven, 200°C/400°F/Gas Mark 6, for 4-5 minutes. Remove and mould over an upturned cup. Leave to set, then cool on a wire rack. Repeat to make 6 cups. Serve the ice cream in the cups.

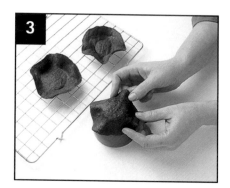

Chocolate Horns with Ginger Cardamom Cream

A crisp chocolate biscuit (cookie) cone encloses a fabulous cardamom-flavoured cream, making this an unusual dessert. You could also serve them as a luxurious teatime treat.

Serves 6

INGREDIENTS

1 egg white
50 g/1³/4 oz/4 tbsp caster (superfine)
   sugar
15 g/¹/2 oz/2 tbsp plain (all-purpose)
   flour
15 g/¹/2 oz/2 tbsp cocoa powder

25 g/1 oz/2 tbsp butter, melted
50 g/1³/4 oz dark chocolate

CARDAMOM CREAM:
150 ml/¹/4 pint/²/3 cup double
   (heavy) cream

1 tbsp icing (confectioners') sugar
¹/4 tsp ground cardamom
pinch of ground ginger
25 g/1 oz stem ginger, chopped finely

1 Place a sheet of baking parchment on 2 baking trays (cookie sheets). Lightly grease 6 cream horn moulds (molds). To make the horns, beat the egg white and sugar in a mixing bowl until well combined. Sieve (strain) the flour and cocoa powder together, then beat into the egg followed by the melted butter.

2 Place 1 tablespoon of the mixture on to 1 baking tray (cookie sheet) and spread out to form a 12.5 cm/5 inch circle. Bake in a preheated oven, 200°C/400°F/ Gas Mark 6, for 4-5 minutes.

3 Working quickly, remove the biscuit (cookie) with a palette knife (spatula) and wrap around the cream horn mould (mold) to form a cone. Leave to set, then remove from the mould (mold). Repeat with the remaining mixture to make 6 cones.

4 Melt the chocolate and dip the open edges of the horn in the chocolate. Place on a piece of baking parchment and leave to set.

5 To make the cardamom cream, place the cream in a bowl and sieve (strain) the icing (confectioners') sugar and ground spices over the surface. Whisk the cream until standing in soft peaks. Fold in the chopped ginger and use to fill the chocolate cones.

Chocolate Charlotte

This chocolate dessert, consisting of a rich chocolate mousse-like filling enclosed in boudoir biscuits (lady-fingers), is a variation of a popular classic.

Serves 8

INGREDIENTS

about 22 boudoir biscuits (lady-fingers)
4 tbsp orange-flavoured liqueur
250 g/9 oz dark chocolate
150 ml/^{1}/$_4$ pint double (heavy) cream
4 eggs

150 g/5^1/$_2$ oz/^{2}/$_3$ cup caster (superfine) sugar

TO DECORATE:
150 ml/^{1}/$_4$ pint/^{2}/$_3$ cup whipping cream

2 tbsp caster (superfine) sugar
^{1}/$_2$ tsp vanilla flavouring (extract)
large dark chocolate curls, (see page 66)
chocolate leaves (see page 44) or chocolate shapes (see page 176)

1 Line the base of a Charlotte mould (mold) or a deep 18 cm/7 inch round cake tin (pan) with a piece of baking parchment.

2 Place the boudoir biscuits (lady-fingers) on a tray and sprinkle with half of the orange-flavoured liqueur. Use to line the sides of the mould (mold) or tin (pan), trimming if necessary to make a tight fit.

3 Break the chocolate into small pieces, place in a bowl and melt over a pan of hot water. Remove from the heat and stir in the double (heavy) cream.

4 Separate the eggs and place the whites in a large grease-free bowl. Beat the egg yolks into the chocolate mixture.

5 Whisk the egg whites until standing in stiff peaks, then gradually add the caster (superfine) sugar, whisking until stiff and glossy. Carefully fold the egg whites into the chocolate mixture in 2 batches, taking care not to knock out all of the air. Pour into the centre of the mould (mold). Trim the biscuits (lady-fingers) so that they are level with the chocolate mixture. Leave to chill for at least 5 hours.

6 To decorate, whisk the cream, sugar and vanilla flavouring (extract) until standing in soft peaks. Turn out the Charlotte on to a serving dish. Pipe cream rosettes around the base and decorate with chocolate curls and leaves.

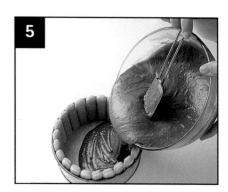

Marble Cheesecake

*A dark and white chocolate cheesecake filling is marbled together
to a give an attractive finish to this rich and decadent dessert.*

Serves 10-12

INGREDIENTS

BASE:
225 g/8 oz toasted oat cereal
50 g/1^3/$_4$ oz/^{1}/$_2$ cup toasted
  hazelnuts, chopped
50 g/1^3/$_4$ oz/4 tbsp butter
25 g/1 oz dark chocolate

FILLING:
350 g/12 oz full fat soft cheese
100 g/3^1/$_2$ oz/7 tbsp caster
  (superfine) sugar
200 ml/7 fl oz/^{3}/$_4$ cup thick yogurt

300 ml/^{1}/$_2$ pint/1^1/$_4$ cups double
  (heavy) cream
1 sachet (envelope) gelatine
3 tbsp water
175 g/6 oz dark chocolate, melted
175 g/6 oz white chocolate, melted

1 Place the toasted oat cereal in a plastic bag and crush with a rolling pin. Pour the crushed cereal into a mixing bowl and stir in the hazelnuts.

2 Melt the butter and chocolate together over a low heat and stir into the cereal mixture, stirring until well coated.

3 Using the bottom of a glass, press the mixture into the base and up the sides of a 20 cm/ 8 inch springform tin (pan).

4 Beat together the cheese and sugar with a wooden spoon until smooth. Beat in the yogurt. Whip the cream until just holding its shape and fold into the mixture. Sprinkle the gelatine over the water in a heatproof bowl and leave to go spongy. Place over a pan of hot water and stir until dissolved. Stir into the mixture.

5 Divide the mixture in half and beat the dark chocolate into one half and the white chocolate into the other half.

6 Place alternate spoonfuls of mixture on top of the cereal base. Swirl the filling together with the tip of a knife to give a marbled effect. Level the top with a scraper or a palette knife (spatula). Leave to chill until set before serving.

COOK'S TIP

For a lighter texture, fold in 2 egg whites whipped to soft peaks before folding in the cream in step 4.

Banana & Coconut Cheesecake

The exotic combination of banana and coconut goes well with chocolate as illustrated in this lovely cheesecake. You can use desiccated (shredded) coconut, but fresh coconut will give a better flavour.

Serves 10

INGREDIENTS

225 g/8 oz chocolate chip cookies
50 g/1³/₄ oz/4 tbsp butter
350 g/12 oz medium-fat soft cheese
75 g/2³/₄ oz/¹/₃ cup caster (superfine) sugar
50 g/1³/₄ oz fresh coconut, grated
2 tbsp coconut-flavoured liqueur

2 ripe bananas
125 g/4¹/₂ oz dark chocolate
1 sachet (envelope) gelatine
3 tbsp water
150 ml/¹/₄ pint/²/₃ cup double (heavy) cream

TO DECORATE:
1 banana
lemon juice
a little melted chocolate

1 Place the biscuits (cookies) in a plastic bag and crush with a rolling pin. Pour into a mixing bowl. Melt the butter and stir into the biscuit (cookie) crumbs until well coated. Firmly press the biscuit (cookie) mixture into the base and up the sides of a 20 cm/ 8 inch springform tin (pan).

2 Beat together the soft cheese and caster (superfine) sugar until well combined, then beat in the grated coconut and coconut-flavoured liqueur. Mash the 2 bananas and beat them in. Melt the dark chocolate and beat in until well combined.

3 Sprinkle the gelatine over the water in a heatproof bowl and leave to go spongy. Place over a pan of hot water and stir until dissolved. Stir into the chocolate mixture. Whisk the cream until just holding its shape and stir into the chocolate mixture. Spoon over the biscuit base and chill until set.

4 To serve, carefully transfer to a serving plate. Slice the banana, toss in the lemon juice and arrange around the edge of the cheesecake. Drizzle with melted chocolate and leave to set.

COOK'S TIP

To crack the coconut, pierce 2 of the 'eyes' and drain off the liquid. Tap hard around the centre with a hammer until it cracks; lever apart.

Chocolate Brandy Torte

A crumbly ginger chocolate base, topped with velvety smooth chocolate brandy cream makes this a blissful cake.

Serves 12

INGREDIENTS

BASE:
250 g/9 oz gingernut biscuits
75 g/2^3/$_4$ oz dark chocolate
100 g/3^1/$_2$ oz/generous ^{1}/$_3$ cup butter

FILLING:
225 g/8 oz dark chocolate

250 g/9 oz mascarpone cheese
2 eggs, separated
3 tbsp brandy
300 ml/^{1}/$_2$ pint/1^1/$_4$ cups double (heavy) cream
50 g/1^3/$_4$ oz/4 tbsp caster (superfine) sugar

TO DECORATE:
100 ml/3^1/$_2$ fl oz/scant ^{1}/$_2$ cup double (heavy) cream
chocolate coffee beans

1 Crush the biscuits in a bag with a rolling pin or in a food processor. Melt the chocolate and butter together and pour over the biscuits. Mix well, then use to line the base and sides of a 23 cm/ 9 inch loose-bottomed fluted flan tin (pan) or springform tin (pan). Leave to chill whilst preparing the filling.

2 To make the filling, melt the dark chocolate in a pan, remove from the heat and beat in the mascarpone cheese, egg yolks and brandy.

3 Lightly whip the cream until just holding its shape and fold in the chocolate mixture.

4 Whisk the egg whites in a grease-free bowl until standing in soft peaks. Add the caster (superfine) sugar a little at a time and whisk until thick and glossy. Fold into the chocolate mixture, in 2 batches, until just mixed.

5 Spoon the mixture into the prepared base and chill for at least 2 hours. Carefully transfer to a serving plate. To decorate, whip the cream and pipe on to the cheesecake and add the chocolate coffee beans.

VARIATION

If chocolate coffee beans are unavailable, use chocolate-coated raisins to decorate.

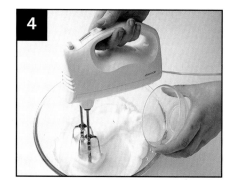

Chocolate Shortcake Towers

Stacks of crisp shortcake are sandwiched together with chocolate-flavoured cream and fresh raspberries, and served with a fresh raspberry coulis.

Serves 6

INGREDIENTS

SHORTCAKE:
225 g/8 oz/1 cup butter
75 g/2 ^{3}/$_4$ oz/^{1}/$_2$ cup light muscovado sugar
50 g/1^3/$_4$ oz dark chocolate, grated
275 g/10^1/$_2$ oz/2^1/$_2$ cups plain (all-purpose) flour

TO FINISH:
350 g/12 oz fresh raspberries
25 g/1 oz/2 tbsp icing (confectioners') sugar
3 tbsp milk
300 ml/^{1}/$_2$ pint/1^1/$_4$ cups double (heavy) cream

100 g/3 oz white chocolate, melted
icing (confectioners') sugar, to dust

1 Lightly grease a baking tray (cookie sheet). To make the shortcake, beat together the butter and sugar until light and fluffy. Beat in the dark chocolate. Mix in the flour to form a stiff dough.

2 Roll out the dough on a lightly floured surface and stamp out eighteen 7.5 cm/3 inch rounds with a fluted biscuit (cookie) cutter. Place the rounds on the baking tray (cookie sheet) and bake in a preheated oven, 200°C/400°F/Gas Mark 6, for 10 minutes until crisp and golden. Leave to cool on the tray (sheet).

3 To make the coulis, set aside about 100 g/3½ oz of the raspberries. Purée the remainder in a food processor with the icing (confectioners') sugar, then push through a sieve to remove the seeds. Chill. Set aside 2 teaspoons of the cream. Whip the remainder until just holding its shape. Fold in the milk and the melted chocolate.

4 For each tower, spoon a little coulis on to a serving plate. Drop small dots of the reserved cream into the coulis around the edge of the plate and use a skewer to drag through the cream to make an attractive pattern.

5 Place a shortcake circle on the plate and spoon on a little of the chocolate cream. Top with 2 or 3 raspberries, top with another shortcake and repeat. Place a third biscuit on top. Dust with sugar.

Black Forest Trifle

*Try all the delightful flavours of a Black Forest Gateau
in this new guise – the results are stunning.*

Serves 6-8

INGREDIENTS

6 thin slices chocolate butter cream
  Swiss roll

2 x 400 g/14 oz can black cherries

2 tbsp kirsch

1 tbsp cornflour (cornstarch)

2 tbsp caster (superfine) sugar

425 ml/$^3/_4$ pint/1$^3/_4$ cups milk

3 egg yolks

1 egg

75 g/2$^3/_4$ oz dark chocolate

300 ml/$^1/_2$ pint/1$^1/_4$ cups double
  (heavy) cream, lightly whipped

TO DECORATE:

dark chocolate, melted

maraschino cherries (optional)

1 Place the slices of chocolate Swiss roll in the bottom of a glass serving bowl.

2 Drain the black cherries, reserving 6 tbsp of the juice. Place the cherries and the reserved juice on top of the cake. Sprinkle with the kirsch.

3 In a bowl, mix the cornflour (cornstarch) and caster (superfine) sugar. Stir in enough of the milk to mix to a smooth paste. Beat in the egg yolks and the whole egg.

4 Heat the remaining milk in a small saucepan until almost boiling, then gradually pour it on to the egg mixture, whisking well until it is combined.

5 Place the bowl over a pan of hot water and cook over a low heat until the custard thickens, stirring. Add the chocolate and stir until melted.

6 Pour the chocolate custard over the cherries and cool. When cold, spread the cream over the custard, swirling with the back of a spoon. Chill before decorating.

7 To make chocolate caraque, spread the melted dark chocolate on a marble or acrylic board. As it begins to set, pull a knife through the chocolate at a 45°C angle, working quickly. Remove each caraque as you make it and chill firmly before using.

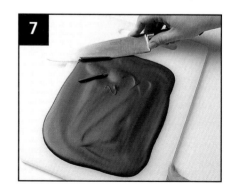

Champagne Mousse

A wonderful champagne-flavoured mouse is served in chocolate sponge cups for an elegant dessert. Any dry sparkling wine made by the traditional method used for champagne can be used.

Serves 4

INGREDIENTS

SPONGE:
4 eggs
100 g/3^1/$_2$ oz/7 tbsp caster
   (superfine) sugar
75 g/2^3/$_4$ oz/^{2}/$_3$ cup self-raising flour
15 g/^{1}/$_4$ oz/2 tbsp cocoa powder
25 g/1 oz/2 tbsp butter, melted

MOUSSE:
1 sachet (envelope) gelatine
3 tbsp water
300 ml/^{1}/$_2$ pint/1^1/$_4$ cups champagne
300 ml/^{1}/$_2$ pint/1^1/$_4$ cups double
   (heavy) cream
2 egg whites

75 g/2^3/$_4$ oz/^{1}/$_3$ cup caster
   (superfine) sugar

TO DECORATE:
50 g/2 oz dark chocolate-flavoured
   cake covering, melted
fresh strawberries

1 Line a 37.5 × 25 cm/15 × 10 inch Swiss roll tin (pan) with greased baking parchment. Place the eggs and sugar in a bowl and whisk with electric beaters until the mixture is very thick and the whisk leaves a trail when lifted. If using a balloon whisk, stand the bowl over a pan of hot water whilst whisking. Sieve (strain) the flour and cocoa together and fold into the egg mixture. Fold in the butter. Pour into the tin (pan) and bake in a preheated oven, 200°C/

400°F/Gas Mark 6, for 8 minutes or until springy to the touch. Cool for 5 minutes, then turn out on to a wire rack until cold. Line four 10 cm/4 inch baking rings with baking parchment. Line the sides with 2.5 cm/1 inch strips of cake and the base with circles.

2 To make the mousse, sprinkle the gelatine over the water and leave to go spongy. Place the bowl over a pan of hot water; stir until dissolved. Stir in the champagne.

3 Whip the cream until just holding its shape. Fold in the champagne mixture. Leave in a cool place until on the point of setting, stirring. Whisk the egg whites until standing in soft peaks, add the sugar and whisk until glossy. Fold into the setting mixture. Spoon into the sponge cases, allowing the mixture to go above the sponge. Chill for 2 hours. Pipe the cake covering in squiggles on a piece of parchment; leave to set. Decorate the mousses.

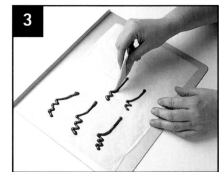

Chocolate Freezer Cake

Hidden in a ring of chocolate cake lies the secret to this freezer cake, a chocolate and mint ice cream. You can use orange or coffee ice cream if preferred.

Serves 8–10

INGREDIENTS

4 eggs
175 g/6 oz/^{3}/$_4$ cup caster (superfine) sugar

100 g/3^1/$_2$ oz/^{3}/$_4$ cup self-raising flour
40 g/1^1/$_2$ oz/3 tbsp cocoa powder

500 ml/^{1}/$_2$ litre/2^1/$_4$ cups chocolate and mint ice cream
Glossy Chocolate Sauce (see page 188)

1 Lightly grease a 23 cm/9 inch ring tin (pan). Place the eggs and sugar in a large mixing bowl. Using an electric whisk if you have one, whisk the mixture until it is very thick and the whisk leaves a trail. If using a balloon whisk, stand the bowl over a pan of hot water whilst whisking.

2 Sieve (strain) the flour and cocoa together and fold into the egg mixture. Pour into the prepared tin (pan) and bake in a preheated oven, 180°C/350°F/Gas Mark 4, for 30 minutes or until springy to the touch. Leave to cool in the tin (pan) before turning out on to a wire rack to cool completely.

3 Rinse the cake tin (pan) and line with a strip of cling film (plastic wrap), overhanging slightly. Cut the top off the cake about 1 cm/^{1}/$_2$ inch thick and set aside.

4 Return the cake to the tin (pan). Using a spoon, scoop out the centre of the cake leaving a shell about 1 cm/^{1}/$_2$ inch thick .

5 Remove the ice cream from the freezer and leave to stand for a few minutes, then beat with a wooden spoon until softened a little. Fill the centre of the cake with the ice cream, levelling the top. Replace the top of the cake.

6 Cover with the overhanging cling film (plastic wrap) and freeze for at least 2 hours.

7 To serve, turn the cake out on to a serving dish and drizzle over some of the chocolate sauce in an attractive pattern, if you wish. Cut the cake into slices and serve the remaining sauce separately.

Mississippi Mud Pie

An all-time favourite with chocoholics – the "mud" refers to the gooey, rich chocolate layer of the cake.

Serves 8-10

INGREDIENTS

225 g/8 oz/2 cups plain (all-purpose)
  flour
25 g/1 oz/^{1}/4 cup cocoa powder
150 g/5^1/2 oz/^{2}/3 cup butter
25 g/1 oz/5 tsp caster (superfine)
  sugar
about 2 tbsp cold water

FILLING:
175 g/6 oz/^{3}/4 cup butter
350 g/12 oz dark muscovado sugar
4 eggs, lightly beaten
4 tbsp cocoa powder, sieved
  (strained)
150 g/5^1/2 oz dark chocolate

300ml/^{1}/2 pt single (light) cream
1 tsp chocolate flavouring (extract)

TO DECORATE:
425 ml/^{3}/4 pint/1^3/4 cups double
  (heavy) cream, whipped
thick bar of chocolate

1 To make the pastry (pie dough), sieve (strain) the flour and cocoa powder into a mixing bowl. Rub in the butter until the mixture resembles fine breadcrumbs. Stir in the sugar and enough cold water to mix to a soft dough. Chill for 15 minutes.

2 Roll out the dough on a lightly floured surface and use to line a deep 23 cm/9 inch loose-bottomed flan tin (pan) or ceramic flan dish. Line with foil or baking parchment and baking beans. Bake blind in a preheated oven, 190°C/375°F/Gas Mark 5, for 15 minutes. Remove the beans and foil or paper and cook for a further 10 minutes until crisp.

3 To make the filling, beat the butter and sugar in a bowl and gradually beat in the eggs with the cocoa powder. Melt the chocolate and beat it into the mixture with the single (light) cream and the chocolate flavouring (extract).

4 Pour the mixture into the cooked pastry case and bake at 170°C/325°F/Gas Mark 3 for 45 minutes or until the filling is set.

5 Leave to cool completely, then transfer the pie to a serving plate, if preferred. Cover with the whipped cream and leave to chill.

6 To make small chocolate curls, use a potato peeler to remove curls from the bar of chocolate. Decorate the pie and leave to chill.

Chocolate Fruit Tartlets

Chocolate pastry trimmed with nuts makes a perfect case (shell) for fruit in these tasty individual tartlets. Use a variety of fruit, either fresh or canned, depending on what is readily available.

Serves 6

INGREDIENTS

250 g/9 oz/1^1/$_4$ cups plain (all-purpose) flour

3 tbsp cocoa powder

150 g/5^1/$_2$ oz/^{2}/$_3$ cup butter

40 g/1^1/$_2$ oz/3 tbsp caster (superfine) sugar

2-3 tbsp water

50 g/1^3/$_4$ oz dark chocolate

50 g/1^3/$_4$ oz/^{1}/$_2$ cup chopped mixed nuts, toasted

350 g/12 oz prepared fruit

3 tbsp apricot jam or redcurrant jelly

1 Sieve (strain) the flour and cocoa powder into a mixing bowl. Cut the butter into small pieces and rub into the flour with your fingertips until the mixture resembles fine breadcrumbs.

2 Stir in the sugar. Add enough of the water to mix to a soft dough, about 1-2 tablespoons. Cover and chill for 15 minutes.

3 Roll out the pastry (pie dough) on a lightly floured surface and use to line six 10 cm/ 4 inch tartlet tins (pans). Prick the pastry (pie dough) with a fork and line the pastry cases (pie shells) with a little crumpled foil. Bake in a preheated oven, 190°C/375°F/ Gas Mark 5, for 10 minutes.

4 Remove the foil and bake for a further 5-10 minutes until the pastry (pie dough) is crisp. Place the tins (pans) on a wire rack to cool completely.

5 Melt the chocolate. Spread out the chopped nuts on a plate. Remove the pastry cases (pie shells) from the tins (pans). Spread melted chocolate on the rims, then dip in the nuts. Leave to set.

6 Arrange the fruit in the tartlet cases (shells). Melt the apricot jam or redcurrant jelly with the remaining 1 tablespoon of water and brush it over the fruit. Chill the tartlets until required.

VARIATION

If liked, you can fill the cases with a little sweetened cream before topping with the fruit. For a chocolate-flavoured filling, blend 225 g/8 oz chocolate hazelnut spread with 5 tablespoons of thick yogurt or whipped cream.

Profiteroles with Banana Cream

Chocolate profiteroles are a popular choice. In this recipe they are filled with a delicious banana-flavoured cream – the perfect combination!

Serves 4-6

INGREDIENTS

CHOUX PASTRY (PIE DOUGH):
150 ml/^{1}/$_4$ pint/^{2}/$_3$ cup water
60 g/2 oz/^{1}/$_4$ cup butter
90 g/3 oz/^{3}/$_4$ cup strong plain (all-purpose) flour, sieved (strained)
2 eggs

CHOCOLATE SAUCE:
100 g/3^1/$_2$ oz dark chocolate, broken into pieces
2 tbsp water
50 g/1^3/$_4$ oz/4 tbsp icing (confectioners') sugar
25 g/1 oz/2 tbsp unsalted butter

FILLING:
300 ml/^{1}/$_2$ pint/1^1/$_4$ cups double (heavy) cream
1 banana
25 g/1 oz/2 tbsp icing (confectioners') sugar
2 tbsp banana-flavoured liqueur

1 Lightly grease a baking tray (cookie sheet) and sprinkle with a little water. To make the pastry, place the water in a pan. Cut the butter into small pieces and add to the pan. Heat gently until the butter melts, then bring to a rolling boil. Remove the pan from the heat and add the flour in one go, beating well until the mixture leaves the sides of the pan and forms a ball. Leave to cool slightly, then gradually beat in the eggs to form a smooth, glossy

mixture. Spoon the paste into a large piping bag fitted with a 1 cm/^{1}/$_2$ inch plain nozzle (tip).

2 Pipe about 18 small balls of the paste on to the baking tray (cookie sheet), allowing enough room for them to expand during cooking. Bake in a preheated oven, 220°C/425°F/Gas Mark 7, for 15-20 minutes until crisp and golden. Remove from the oven and make a small slit in each one for steam to escape. Cool on a wire rack.

3 To make the sauce, place all the ingredients in a heatproof bowl, set over a pan of simmering water and heat until combined to make a smooth sauce, stirring.

4 To make the filling, whip the cream until standing in soft peaks. Mash the banana with the sugar and liqueur. Fold into the cream. Place in a piping bag fitted with a 1 cm/^{1}/$_2$ inch plain nozzle (tip) and pipe into the profiteroles. Serve with the sauce poured over.

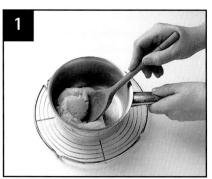

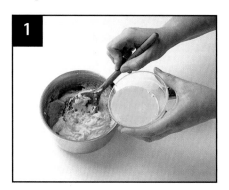

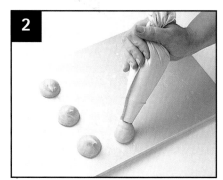

Sweets & Drinks

There is nothing quite as nice as home-made chocolates and sweets – they leave the average box of chocolates in the shade!

You'll find recipes in this chapter to suit everybody's taste. Wonderful, rich, melt-in-the-mouth chocolate truffles, crispy florentines, nutty chocolate creams and rich chocolate liqueurs – they're all here. There is even some simple-to-make chocolate fudge, so there is no need to fiddle about with sugar thermometers.

Looking for something to wash it all down? We have included two delightfully cool summer chocolate drinks and for warmth and comfort on winter nights two hot drinks that will simply put instant hot chocolate to shame. Enjoy!

Rocky Road Bites

Young children will love these chewy bites. You can vary the ingredients and use different nuts and dried fruit according to taste.

Makes 18

INGREDIENTS

125 g/4¹/2 oz milk chocolate
50 g/2¹/2 oz mini multi-coloured
  marshmallows

25 g/1 oz/¹/4 cup chopped walnuts

25 g/1 oz no-soak apricots, chopped

1 Line a baking tray (cookie sheet) with baking parchment and set aside.

2 Break the milk chocolate into small pieces and place in a large mixing bowl. Set the bowl over a pan of simmering water and stir until the chocolate has melted.

3 Stir in the marshmallows, walnuts and apricots and toss in the melted chocolate until well covered.

4 Place heaped teaspoons of the mixture on to the prepared baking tray (cookie sheet).

5 Leave the sweets (candies) to chill in the refrigerator until set.

6 Once set, carefully remove the sweets from the baking parchment.

7 The chewy bites can be placed in paper sweet (candy) cases to serve, if desired.

COOK'S TIP

These sweets (candies) can be stored in a cool, dry place for up to 2 weeks.

VARIATION

Light, fluffy marshmallows are available in white or pastel colours. If you cannot find mini marshmallows, use large ones and snip them into smaller pieces with kitchen scissors before mixing them into the melted chocolate in step 3.

Easy Chocolate Fudge

This is the easiest fudge to make – for a really rich flavour, use a good dark chocolate with a high cocoa content, ideally at least 70 per cent.

Makes 25–30 pieces

INGREDIENTS

500 g/1 lb 2 oz dark chocolate
75 g/2³/₄ oz/¹/₃ cup unsalted butter

400 g/14 oz can sweetened
condensed milk

¹/₂ tsp vanilla flavouring (extract)

1 Lightly grease a 20 cm/8 inch square cake tin (pan).

2 Break the chocolate into pieces and place in a large saucepan with the butter and condensed milk.

3 Heat gently, stirring until the chocolate and butter melts and the mixture is smooth. Do not allow to boil.

4 Remove from the heat. Beat in the vanilla flavouring (extract), then beat the mixture for a few minutes until thickened. Pour it into the prepared tin (pan) and level the top.

5 Chill the mixture in the refrigerator until firm.

6 Tip the fudge out on to a chopping board and cut into squares to serve.

VARIATION

For chocolate peanut fudge, replace 50 g/1¹/₂ oz/4 tbsp of the butter with crunchy peanut butter.

COOK'S TIP

Don't use milk chocolate as the results will be too sticky.

COOK'S TIP

Store the fudge in an airtight container in a cool, dry place for up to 1 month. Do not freeze.

No-Cook Fruit & Nut Chocolate Fudge

Chocolate, nuts and dried fruit – the perfect combination – are all found in this simple-to-make fudge.

Makes about 25 pieces

INGREDIENTS

250 g/9 oz dark chocolate
25 g/1 oz/2 tbsp butter
4 tbsp evaporated milk

450 g/1 lb/3 cups icing (confectioners') sugar, sieved (strained)

50 g/1³/4 oz/¹/2 cup roughly chopped hazelnuts
50 g/1³/4 oz/¹/3 cup sultanas (golden raisins)

1 Lightly grease a 20 cm/8 inch square cake tin (pan).

2 Break the chocolate into pieces and place it in a bowl with the butter and evaporated milk. Set the bowl over a pan of gently simmering water and stir until the chocolate and butter have melted and the ingredients are well combined.

3 Remove the bowl from the heat and gradually beat in the icing (confectioners') sugar. Stir the hazelnuts and sultanas (golden raisins) into the mixture. Press the fudge into the prepared tin (pan) and level the top. Chill until firm.

4 Tip the fudge out on to a chopping board and cut into squares. Place in paper sweet (candy) cases. Chill until required.

COOK'S TIP

The fudge can be stored in an airtight container for up to 2 weeks.

VARIATION

Vary the nuts used in this recipe; try making the fudge with almonds, brazil nuts, walnuts or pecans.

Nutty Chocolate Clusters

*Nuts and crisp biscuits (cookies) encased in chocolate make
these sweets (candy) rich, chocolatey and quite irresistible!*

Makes about 30

INGREDIENTS

175 g/6 oz white chocolate
100 g/3$^{1}/_{2}$ oz digestive biscuits
(graham crackers)

100 g/3$^{1}/_{2}$ oz macadamia nuts or
brazil nuts, chopped

25 g/1 oz stem ginger, chopped
(optional)
175 g/6 oz dark chocolate

1 Line a baking tray (cookie sheet) with a sheet of baking parchment. Break the white chocolate into small pieces and place in a large mixing bowl set over a pan of gently simmering water; stir until melted.

2 Break the digestive biscuits (graham crackers) into small pieces. Stir the biscuits (graham crackers) into the melted chocolate with the chopped nuts and stem ginger, if using.

3 Place heaped teaspoons of the mixture on to the prepared baking tray (cookie sheet).

4 Chill the mixture until set, then carefully remove from the baking parchment.

5 Melt the dark chocolate and leave it to cool slightly. Dip the clusters into the melted chocolate, allowing the excess to drip back into the bowl. Return the clusters to the baking tray (cookie sheet) and chill in the refrigerator until set.

COOK'S TIP

*The clusters can be stored for up to
1 week in a cool, dry place.*

COOK'S TIP

*Macadamia and brazil nuts are
both rich and high in fat, which
makes them particularly popular for
confectionery, but other nuts can be
used, if preferred.*

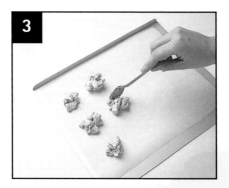

Chocolate Cherries

These tasty cherry and marzipan sweets (candy) are simple to make. Serve as petits fours
at the end of a meal or for an indulgent nibble at any time of the day.

Makes 24

INGREDIENTS

12 glacé (candied) cherries
2 tbsp rum or brandy

250 g/9 oz marzipan
125 g/5¹/₂ oz dark chocolate

extra milk, dark or white chocolate,
to decorate (optional)

1 Line a baking tray (cookie sheet) with a sheet of baking parchment.

2 Cut the cherries in half and place in a small bowl. Add the rum or brandy and stir to coat. Leave the cherries to soak for at least 1 hour, stirring occasionally.

3 Divide the marzipan into 24 pieces and roll each piece into a ball. Press half a cherry into the top of each marzipan ball.

4 Break the chocolate into pieces, place in a bowl and set over a pan of hot water. Stir until the chocolate has melted.

5 Dip each sweet (candy) into the melted chocolate, allowing the excess to drip back into the bowl. Place the coated cherries on the baking parchment and chill until set.

6 If liked, melt a little extra chocolate and drizzle it over the top of the coated cherries. Leave to set.

VARIATION

Flatten the marzipan and use it to mould (mold) around the cherries to cover them, then dip in the chocolate as above.

VARIATION

Use a whole almond in place of the halved glacé (candied) cherries and omit the rum or brandy.

Chocolate Marzipans

These delightful little morsels make the perfect gift,
if you can resist eating them all yourself!

Makes about 30

INGREDIENTS

450 g/1 lb marzipan
25 g/1 oz/⅓ cup glacé (candied)
  cherries, chopped very finely
25 g/1 oz stem ginger, chopped very
  finely

50 g/1¾ oz no-soak dried apricots,
  chopped very finely
350 g/12 oz dark chocolate
25 g/1 oz white chocolate

icing (confectioners') sugar, to dust

1 Line a baking tray (cookie sheet) with a sheet of baking parchment. Divide the marzipan into 3 balls and knead each ball to soften it.

2 Work the glacé (candied) cherries into one portion of the marzipan by kneading on a surface lightly dusted with icing (confectioners') sugar.

3 Do the same with the stem ginger and another portion of marzipan and then the apricots and the third portion of marzipan.

4 Form each flavoured portion of marzipan into small balls, keeping the different flavours separate.

5 Melt the dark chocolate. Dip one of each flavoured ball of marzipan into the chocolate by spiking each one with a cocktail stick (toothpick) or small skewer, allowing the excess chocolate to drip back into the bowl.

6 Carefully place the balls in clusters of the three flavours on the prepared baking tray (cookie sheet). Repeat with the remaining marzipan balls. Chill until set.

7 Melt the white chocolate and drizzle a little over the tops of each cluster of marzipan balls. Chill until hardened, then remove from the baking parchment and dust with sugar to serve.

VARIATION

Coat the marzipan balls in white or milk chocolate and drizzle with dark chocolate, if you prefer.

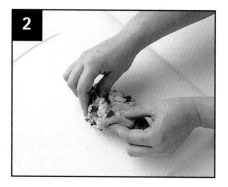

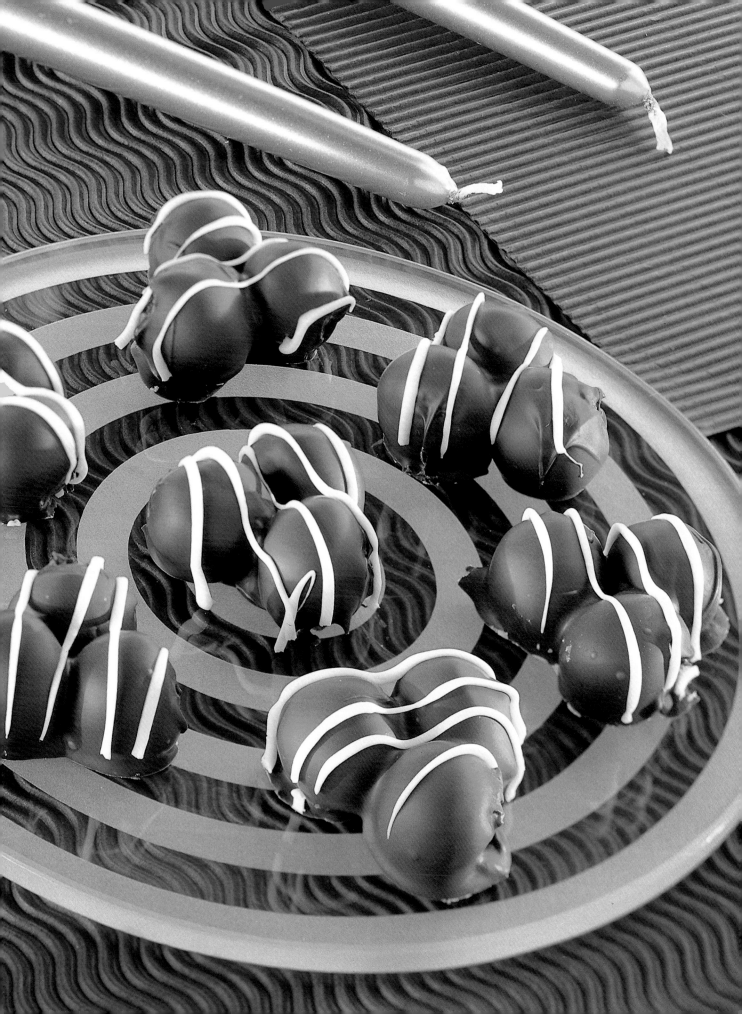

Chocolate Liqueurs

These tasty chocolate cups are filled with a delicious liqueur-flavoured filling. They are a little fiddly to make but lots of fun! Use your favourite liqueur to flavour the cream.

Makes 20

INGREDIENTS

100 g/3^1/2 oz dark chocolate
about 5 glacé (candied) cherries,
  halved
about 10 hazelnuts or macadamia
  nuts

150 ml/^{1}/4 pint/^{2}/3 cup double
  (heavy) cream
25 g/1 oz/2 tbsp icing
  (confectioners') sugar
4 tbsps liqueur

TO FINISH:
50 g/1^3/4 oz dark chocolate, melted
a little white chocolate, melted or
  white chocolate curls (see page 66)
  or extra nuts and cherries

1 Line a baking tray (cookie sheet) with a sheet of baking parchment. Melt the chocolate and spoon it into 20 paper sweet (candy) cases, spreading up the sides with a small spoon or pastry brush. Place upside down on the prepared baking tray (cookie sheet) and leave to set.

2 Carefully peel away the paper cases. Place a cherry or nut in the base of each cup.

3 To make the filling, place the double (heavy) cream in a mixing bowl and sieve (strain) the icing (confectioners') sugar on top. Whisk the cream until it is just holding its shape, then whisk in the liqueur.

4 Place the cream in a piping bag fitted with a 1 cm/^{1}/2 inch plain nozzle (tip) and pipe a little into each chocolate case. Leave to chill for 20 minutes.

5 To finish, spoon the melted dark chocolate over the cream to cover it and pipe the melted white chocolate on top, swirling it into the dark chocolate with a cocktail stick (toothpick). Leave to harden. Alternatively, cover the cream with the melted dark chocolate and decorate with white chocolate curls before setting. Or, place a small piece of nut or cherry on top of the cream and then cover with dark chocolate.

COOK'S TIP

Sweet (candy) cases can vary in size. Use the smallest you can find for this recipe.

Chocolate Cups with Mascarpone Filling

Mascarpone – the velvety smooth Italian cheese – makes a rich, creamy filling for these tasty chocolates

Makes 20

INGREDIENTS

100 g/3¹/₂ oz dark chocolate

FILLING:
100 g/3¹/₂ oz milk or dark chocolate
¹/₄ tsp vanilla flavouring (extract)

200 g/7 oz mascarpone cheese
cocoa powder, to dust

1 Line a baking tray (cookie sheet) with a sheet of baking parchment. Melt the chocolate and spoon it into 20 paper sweet (candy) cases, spreading up the sides with a small spoon or pastry brush. Place upside down on the prepared baking tray (cookie sheet) and leave to set.

2 When set, carefully peel away the paper cases.

3 To make the filling, melt the dark or milk chocolate. Place the mascarpone cheese in a bowl and beat in the vanilla flavouring (extract) and melted chocolate and beat until well combined. Leave the mixture to chill, beating occasionally until firm enough to pipe.

4 Place the mascarpone filling in a piping bag fitted with a star nozzle (tip) and pipe the mixture into the cups. Decorate with a dusting of cocoa powder.

COOK'S TIP

Mascarpone is a rich Italian soft cheese made from fresh cream, so it has a high fat content. Its delicate flavour blends well with chocolate.

VARIATION

You can use lightly whipped double (heavy) cream instead of the mascarpone cheese, if preferred.

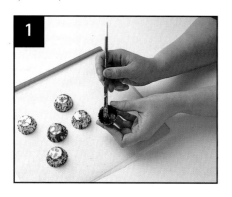

Mini Chocolate Cones

These unusual cone-shaped chocolates make an interesting change from the more usual cup shape.
Filled with a mint-flavoured cream, they are perfect for an after-dinner chocolate.

Makes 10

INGREDIENTS

75 g/2³/4 oz dark chocolate
100 ml/3¹/2 fl oz/¹/3 cup double
(heavy) cream

15 g/¹/2 oz/1 tbsp icing
(confectioners') sugar
1 tbsp crème de menthe

chocolate coffee beans, to decorate
(optional)

1 Cut ten 7.5 cm/3 inch circles of baking parchment. Shape each circle into a cone shape and secure with sticky tape.

2 Melt the chocolate. Using a small pastry brush or clean artists' brush, brush the inside of each cone with melted chocolate.

3 Brush a second layer of chocolate on the inside of the cones and leave to chill until set. Carefully peel away the paper.

4 Place the double (heavy) cream, icing (confectioners') sugar and crème de menthe in a mixing bowl and whip until just holding its shape. Place in a piping bag fitted with a star nozzle (tip) and pipe the mixture into the chocolate cones.

5 Decorate the cones with chocolate coffee beans (if using) and chill until required.

COOK'S TIP

The chocolate cones can be made in advance and kept in the refrigerator for up to 1 week. Do not fill them more than 2 hours before you are going to serve them.

VARIATION

Use a different flavoured liqueur to flavour the cream: a coffee-flavoured liqueur is perfect. If you want a mint flavour without using a liqueur, use a few drops of peppermint flavouring (extract) to flavour the cream according to taste.

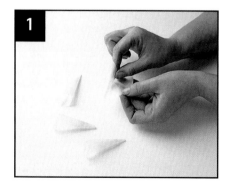

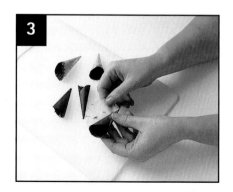

Collettes

A creamy, orange-flavoured chocolate filling in white chocolate cups makes a wonderful treat.

Makes 20

INGREDIENTS

100 g/3¹/₂ oz white chocolate

FILLING:
150 g/5¹/₂ oz orange-flavoured dark chocolate
150 ml/¹/₄ pint/²/₃ cup double (heavy) cream

25 g/1 oz/2 tbsp icing (confectioners') sugar

1 Line a baking tray (cookie sheet) with a sheet of baking parchment. Melt the chocolate and spoon it into 20 paper sweet (candy) cases, spreading up the sides with a small spoon or pastry brush. Place upside down on the prepared baking tray (cookie sheet) and leave to set.

2 When set, carefully peel away the paper cases.

3 To make the filling, melt the orange-flavoured chocolate and place in a mixing bowl with the double (heavy) cream and the icing (confectioners') sugar. Beat until smooth. Chill until the mixture becomes firm enough to pipe, stirring occasionally.

4 Place the filling in a piping bag fitted with a star nozzle (tip) and pipe a little into each case. Leave to chill until required.

COOK'S TIP

Use the smallest sweet (candy) cases you can find for these cups.

COOK'S TIP

If they do not hold their shape well, use 2 cases to make a double thickness mould (mold). Foil cases are firmer so use these if you can find them.

VARIATION

Add 1 tbsp orange-flavoured liqueur to the filling, if preferred.

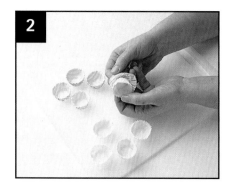

Mini Florentines

These classic biscuits (cookies) can be served with desserts but they also make delightful petits fours. Serve at the end of a meal with coffee, or arrange in a shallow presentation box for an attractive gift.

Makes about 40

INGREDIENTS

75 g/2³/4 oz/¹/3 cup butter
75 g/2³/4 oz/¹/3 cup caster (superfine) sugar
25 g/1 oz/2 tbsp sultanas (golden raisins) or raisins

25 g/1 oz/2 tbsp glacé (candied) cherries, chopped
25 g/1 oz/2 tbsp crystallised ginger, chopped
25 g/1 oz sunflower seeds

100 g/3¹/2 oz/³/4 cup flaked (slivered) almonds
2 tbsp double (heavy) cream
175 g/6 oz dark or milk chocolate

1 Lightly grease and flour 2 baking trays (cookie sheets) or line with baking parchment. Place the butter in a small pan and heat gently until melted. Add the sugar, stir until dissolved, then bring the mixture to the boil. Remove from the heat and stir in the sultanas (golden raisins) or raisins, cherries, ginger, sunflower seeds and almonds. Mix well, then beat in the cream.

2 Place small teaspoons of the fruit and nut mixture on to the prepared baking tray (cookie sheet), allowing plenty of space for the mixture to spread. Bake in a preheated oven, 180°C/350°F/Gas Mark 4, for 10-12 minutes until light golden in colour.

3 Remove from the oven and, whilst still hot, use a circular biscuit (cookie) cutter to pull in the edges to form a perfect circle. Leave to cool and crispen before removing from the baking tray (cookie sheet).

4 Melt most of the chocolate and spread it on a sheet of baking parchment. When the chocolate is on the point of setting, place the biscuits (cookies) flat-side down on the chocolate and leave to harden completely.

5 Cut around the florentines and remove from the paper. Spread a little more chocolate on the already coated side of the florentines and use a fork to mark waves in the chocolate. Leave to set. Arrange the florentines on a plate (or in a presentation box for a gift) with alternate sides facing upwards. Keep cool.

Mini Chocolate Tartlets

Small pastry cases (pie shells) are filled with a rich chocolate filling to serve as petits fours. Use mini muffin tins (pans) or small individual tartlet tins (pans) to make the pastry cases (pie shells).

Makes about 18

INGREDIENTS

175 g/6 oz/1^1/$_2$ cups plain (all-purpose) flour
75 g 2^3/$_4$ oz/^{1}/$_3$ cup butter
15 g/^{1}/$_2$ oz/1 tbsp caster (superfine) sugar
about 1 tbsp water

FILLING:
100 g/3^1/$_2$ oz full-fat soft cheese
25 g/1 oz/5 tsp caster (superfine) sugar
1 small egg, lightly beaten
50 g/1^3/$_4$ oz dark chocolate

TO DECORATE:
100 ml/3^1/$_2$ fl oz/^{1}/$_3$ cup double (heavy) cream
dark chocolate curls (see page 214)
cocoa powder, to dust

1 Sieve (strain) the flour into a mixing bowl. Cut the butter into small pieces and rub in with your fingertips until the mixture resembles fine breadcrumbs. Stir in the sugar. Add enough water to mix to a soft dough, then cover and chill for 15 minutes.

2 Roll out the pastry (pie dough) on a lightly floured surface and use to line 18 mini tartlet tins (pans) or mini muffin tins (pans). Prick the bases with a cocktail stick (toothpick).

3 Beat together the full-fat soft cheese and the sugar. Beat in the egg. Melt the chocolate and beat it into the mixture. Spoon into the pastry cases (pie shells) and bake in a preheated oven, 190°C/375°F/Gas Mark 5, for 15 minutes until the pastry (pie dough) is crisp and the filling set. Place the tins (pans) on a wire rack to cool completely.

4 Chill the tartlets. Whip the cream until it is just holding its shape. Place in a piping bag fitted with a star nozzle (tip). Pipe rosettes of cream on top of the tartlets. Decorate with chocolate curls and dust with cocoa powder.

COOK'S TIP

The tartlets can be made up to 3 days ahead. Decorate on the day of serving, preferably no more than 4 hours in advance.

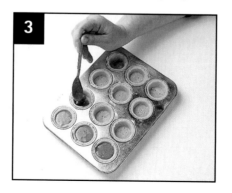

Rum Truffles

Truffles are always popular. They make a fabulous gift or,
served with coffee, they are a perfect end to a meal.

Makes about 20

INGREDIENTS

125 g/5¹/₂ oz dark chocolate
small knob of butter
2 tbsp rum

50 g/1³/₄ oz desiccated (shredded)
coconut
100 g/3¹/₂ oz cake crumbs

75 g/2³/₄ oz/6 tbsp icing
(confectioners') sugar
2 tbsp cocoa powder

1 Break the chocolate into pieces and place in a bowl with the butter. Set the bowl over a pan of gently simmering water, stir until melted and combined.

2 Remove from the heat and beat in the rum. Stir in the desiccated (shredded) coconut, cake crumbs and 50 g/1³/₄ oz of the icing (confectioners') sugar. Beat until combined. Add a little extra rum if the mixture is stiff.

3 Roll the mixture into small balls and place them on a sheet of baking parchment. Leave to chill until firm.

4 Sieve (strain) the remaining icing (confectioners') sugar on to a large plate. Sieve (strain) the cocoa powder on to another plate. Roll half of the truffles in the icing (confectioners') sugar until coated and roll the remaining truffles in the cocoa powder.

5 Place the truffles in paper sweet (candy) cases and leave to chill until required.

COOK'S TIP

These truffles will keep for about
2 weeks in a cool place.

VARIATION

Make the truffles with
white chocolate and
replace the rum with
coconut liqueur or milk, if you
prefer. Roll them in cocoa powder or
dip in melted milk chocolate.

White Chocolate Truffles

These delicious creamy white truffles will testify to the fact that there is nothing quite as nice as home-made chocolates. It is worth buying the best chocolate you can for these truffles.

Makes about 20

INGREDIENTS

25 g/1 oz/2 tbsp unsalted
  butter
75 ml/3 fl oz/5 tbsp double (heavy)
  cream

225 g/8 oz good quality Swiss white
  chocolate
1 tbsp orange-flavoured liqueur
  (optional)

TO FINISH:
100 g/3$^1/_2$ oz white chocolate

1 Line a Swiss roll tin (pan) with baking parchment.

2 Place the butter and cream in a small saucepan and bring slowly to the boil, stirring constantly. Boil for 1 minute, then remove from the heat.

3 Break the chocolate into pieces and add to the cream. Stir until melted, then beat in the liqueur, if using.

4 Pour into the prepared tin (pan) and chill for about 2 hours until firm.

5 Break off pieces of mixture and roll them into balls. Chill for a further 30 minutes before finishing the truffles.

6 To finish, melt the white chocolate. Dip the balls in the chocolate, allowing the excess to drip back into the bowl. Place on non-stick baking parchment and swirl the chocolate with the prongs of a fork. Leave to harden.

7 Drizzle a little melted dark chocolate over the truffles if you wish and leave to set. Place the truffles in paper cases to serve.

COOK'S TIP

The truffle mixture needs to be firm but not too hard to roll. If the mixture is too hard, allow it to stand at room temperature for a few minutes to soften slightly. During rolling the mixture will become sticky but will reharden in the refrigerator before coating.

COOK'S TIP

The chocolates can be kept in the refrigerator for up to 2 weeks.

Italian Chocolate Truffles

These tasty little morsels are flavoured with almonds and chocolate, and are simplicity itself to make. Served with coffee, they are the perfect end to a meal.

Makes about 24

INGREDIENTS

175 g/6 oz dark chocolate
2 tbsp almond-flavoured liqueur (amaretto) or orange-flavoured liqueur

40 g/1^1/2 oz/3 tbsp unsalted butter
50 g/1^3/4 oz icing (confectioners') sugar

50 g/1^3/4 oz/^{1}/2 cup ground almonds
50 g/1^3/4 oz grated chocolate

1 Melt the dark chocolate with the liqueur in a bowl set over a saucepan of hot water, stirring until well combined.

2 Add the butter and stir until it has melted. Stir in the icing (confectioners') sugar and the ground almonds.

3 Leave the mixture in a cool place until firm enough to roll into about 24 balls.

4 Place the grated chocolate on a plate and roll the truffles in the chocolate to coat them.

5 Place the truffles in paper sweet (candy) cases and chill.

COOK'S TIP

These truffles will keep for about 2 weeks in a cool place.

VARIATION

The almond-flavoured liqueur gives these truffles an authentic Italian flavour. The original almond liqueur, Amaretto di Saronno, comes from Saronno in Italy.

VARIATION

For a sweeter truffle, use milk chocolate instead of dark. Dip the truffles in melted chocolate to finish, if desired.

Hot Chocolate Drinks

*Rich and soothing, a hot chocolate drink in the evening can be just
what you need to help ease away the stresses of the day.*

Serves 2

INGREDIENTS

SPICY HOT CHOCOLATE:
600 ml/1 pint/2^1/$_2$ cups milk
1 tsp ground mixed spice
   (allspice)
100 g/3^1/$_2$ oz dark chocolate
4 cinnamon sticks

100 ml/3^1/$_2$ fl oz/^{1}/$_3$ cup double
(heavy) cream, lightly whipped

HOT CHOCOLATE & ORANGE TODDY:
75 g/2^1/$_2$ oz orange-flavoured dark
chocolate

600 ml/1 pint/2^1/$_2$ cups milk
3 tbsp rum
2 tbsp double (heavy) cream
grated nutmeg

1 To make Spicy Hot
Chocolate, pour the milk into
a small pan. Sprinkle in the mixed
spice (allspice).

2 Break the dark chocolate into
squares and add to the milk.
Heat the mixture over a low heat
until the milk is just boiling,
stirring all the time to prevent the
milk burning on the bottom of
the pan.

3 Place 2 cinnamon sticks in
2 cups and pour in the spicy

hot chocolate. Top with the
whipped double (heavy) cream
and serve.

4 To make Hot Chocolate &
Orange Toddy, break the
orange-flavoured dark chocolate
into squares and place in a small
saucepan with the milk. Heat over
a low heat until just boiling,
stirring constantly.

5 Remove the pan from the
heat and stir in the rum.
Pour into cups.

6 Pour the cream over the back
of a spoon or swirl on to the
top so that it sits on top of the hot
chocolate. Sprinkle with grated
nutmeg and serve at once.

COOK'S TIP

*Using a cinnamon stick as
a stirrer will give any
hot chocolate drink a
sweet, pungent flavour of cinnamon
without overpowering the flavour
of the chocolate.*

Cold Chocolate Drinks

*These delicious chocolate summer drinks are perfect for
making a chocoholic's summer day!*

Serves 2

INGREDIENTS

CHOCOLATE MILK SHAKE:
450 ml/16 fl oz/2 cups ice cold
  milk
3 tbsp drinking chocolate powder
3 scoops chocolate ice cream

cocoa powder, to dust (optional)

CHOCOLATE ICE CREAM SODA:
5 tbsp chocolate dessert sauce
soda water

2 scoops of chocolate ice cream
double (heavy) cream, whipped
dark or milk chocolate, grated

1 To make Chocolate Milk Shake, place half of the ice-cold milk in a blender.

2 Add the drinking chocolate powder to the blender and 1 scoop of the chocolate ice cream. Blend until the mixture is frothy and well mixed. Stir in the remaining milk.

3 Place the remaining 2 scoops of chocolate ice cream in 2 serving glasses and carefully pour the chocolate milk over the ice cream.

4 Sprinkle a little cocoa powder (if using) over the top of each drink and serve at once.

5 To make Chocolate Ice Cream Soda, divide the chocolate dessert sauce between 2 glasses. (You can use a ready-made chocolate dessert sauce, or the Hot Chocolate Sauce on page 160, or the Glossy Chocolate Sauce on page 188.)

6 Add a little soda water to each glass and stir to combine the sauce and soda water. Place a scoop of ice cream in each glass and top up with more soda water.

7 Place a dollop of whipped heavy (double) cream on the top, if liked, and sprinkle with a little grated dark or milk chocolate.

COOK'S TIP

*Served in a tall glass, a milk shake
or an ice cream soda makes a
scrumptious snack in a drink.
Serve with straws, if wished.*

Index

Index compiled by Hilary Bird.